Strategic Meetings Management Handbook

FROM THEORY TO PRACTICE

Strategic Meetings Management Handbook

FROM THEORY TO PRACTICE

Edited by
Kevin Iwamoto

WITH EDITORIAL ASSISTANCE BY DON MUNRO

easton studio
press

Easton Studio Press
PO Box 3131
Westport, CT 06880
203 454-4454
www.eastonsp.com

Book production by Creative Management Partners
Book design by Barbara Aronica-Buck

Hardcover ISBN: 978-1-935212-54-6
E-book ISBN: 978-1-935212-53-9

First edition
Printed in the United States of America

First printing: August 2011
10 9 8 7 6 5 4 3 2 1

CONTENTS

CONTENTS

ACKNOWLEDGMENTS

StarCite is proud to support the publication of the *Strategic Meetings Management Handbook: From Theory to Practice*, which brings together the collective knowledge of many of the meetings industry's visionaries, pioneers, and foremost practitioners.

Throughout its decade-plus history, StarCite's innovation in technology has moved forward alongside development of a best-practice road map. This road map incorporates the leading strategies developed and deployed with our forward-thinking clients and partners, benchmarking and research from the meetings data we've collected, policies developed by industry groups, and the ideas brought forth by StarCite's many talented employees.

While StarCite is a meetings technology company, technology is purely an enabler—many other driving forces such as policy, strategy, change management, vision, and leadership are necessary to deploy an effective strategic meetings management program.

ACKNOWLEDGMENTS

Several other people came together to help this book come to life. They include Connor Gray, Mary McDaniel, and Christine Ottow for editorial assistance. Thanks also to Martha Brooks for illustration and cover image design.

This handbook will serve as a new source of advice to travel, meeting, and procurement professionals around the world who wish to bring the benefits of strategic meetings management to their organizations.

FOREWORD

Welcome to *Strategic Meetings Management Handbook: From Theory to Practice*. This book offers the experience and perspective of eleven of the meetings industry's leading experts and observers from around the world. These individuals have lived both the theory of strategic meetings management and the practical *application* of that theory.

This is unlike any book covering the corporate meetings industry today. We didn't set out to define strategic meetings management. There is plenty of research in the industry today that you can use to help you do that. Rather, we hope you will consider this book a comprehensive go-to resource on the application of the theory and practice of strategic meetings management (SMM) in the context of select topics. Each chapter is intended to standalone so that you can use each one separately. However, as a collection it is a comprehensive practitioner's guide to strategic meetings management.

Enjoy reading this handbook. The topics and authors will stimulate your thoughts and help you move forward with confidence with your strategic meetings management program. Thus you will bring positive impact to your company's bottom line, improve service levels to internal customers and attendees, and win recognition of excellence from senior management.

Strategic Meetings Management Handbook

FROM THEORY TO PRACTICE

The original impetus behind the creation of the strategic meetings management program (SMMP) mirrors many organizations' adoption of the theory today. Kevin Iwamoto, global leadership professional (GLP) and vice president of enterprise strategy at StarCite, provides insight into his personal journey into the development of the theory and practice. The trail blazed has provided a road map that countless companies now use in pursuing an organized, efficient, and successful meetings and events program. Using an SMMP, companies are able to gain visibility into meetings that are occurring, leverage proven supplier management techniques, and place controls at the appropriate points of the processes.

Origins of the Theory:

Payoff from the Practice

by Kevin Iwamoto

The most successful businessman is the man who holds onto the old just as long as it is good, and grabs the new just as soon as it is better.

— Robert P. Vanderpoel

It is well documented that one of the largest areas of "unmanaged" corporate spend is meetings and events functions. This sector typically represents 1%–3% of corporate revenue, and until fairly recently was often treated as isolated independent projects, without documented policy, handled by a myriad of personnel. But in this era of enhanced budgetary scrutiny, human capital reduction, and economic upheaval, global industry leaders have embraced a new philosophy, methodology and process: strategic meetings management.

In this book, StarCite has gathered eleven thought leaders from around the business travel and meetings industry to discuss various elements of strategic meetings management (SMM) and how it can:

- Align with your organization's strategic goals and vision
- Increase visibility of your meetings spend
- Save money and bolster control over expenditures
- Improve process efficiencies
- Raise service levels to meetings attendees
- Boost leverage with suppliers
- Mitigate risk

While an SMMP can help you with all these goals, there is often resistance within an organization, with bias toward already established ways of planning and managing events, as well as any home-grown program of managing meetings activities and spend. In many cases, such as in a decentralized environment, multiple planners (some untrained) source for venues manually in very inefficient ways; use their own favored suppliers; pay for services in a variety of ways (including personal cards); sign contracts worth thousands of dollars; and fail to track valuable meetings data that can be used to improve control and elevate buying power.

There's a better way—strategic meetings management—a holistic, centralized, automated, and more efficient way of managing all of a firm's meetings and events activities and spend. This book contains the wisdom of the leading industry experts and presents concepts about SMM and its rewards that you can then apply within your own organization.

SMMP: A History of Collaboration

With the publication of this book, I can't help but reflect on my journey along the road leading to the creation of SMM. First, never in a million years did I think I'd have anything to do with a doctrine or new processes of how meetings should be managed. My journey was a circuitous one. It began out of my desire to help address the burgeoning need among companies for a road map to manage groups and meetings—the "last frontier" of managed travel spend; I also wanted to assist direct corporate members of the Global Business Travel Association (GBTA) who were increasingly inheriting responsibility for their company meetings and were unfamiliar about the groups and meetings marketplace. Ultimately, and ironically, the journey ended with SMM serving my own needs at Hewlett-Packard where, as senior global commodity manager, I inherited responsibilities for the global HP Smart Meetings program, which had been launched by my predecessors in North America and Europe; my assignment was to improve the SMMP model and to complete the global launch in Asia-Pacific.

For me, it all started in 2003, when I was winding down my two-year stint as president and CEO of GBTA (then the National Business Travel Association) and its foundation arm. It was an extremely rewarding post but also very challenging. The association and many of its members were still struggling during an economic slowdown that began after the tragedy of September 11. During my leadership at GBTA, I noticed that I was having more and more conversations with travel and procurement managers who, due to budget cuts at their organizations, had been given the responsibility to centralize management of *all* travel spend categories to gain the greatest possible savings and efficiencies.

For most, that meant they suddenly had to get some kind of idea of the organization-wide extent of their meetings and incentive spending. And so, travel managers were reaching out, asking, "How can GBTA help me learn about this new category of spend that I'm managing? And where do I go to get access to information, resources and training?" They needed guidance on issues such as:

- Providing a single view of all meetings held across the organization
- Facilitating meeting execution and management
- Leveraging buying power, reducing expenses, eliminating inefficiencies
- Gaining visibility of unmanaged spend
- Reducing risk
- Assuring compliance

There were few readily available answers. I was no expert on meetings management. I was, however, very experienced in overseeing development, policy creation, strategy, and supplier management for various global travel spend categories at HP. But at that time, I didn't oversee meetings management.

Obstacles, Then Success

The decision to start the SMM ball rolling was not without its roadblocks and the kind of resistance one often encounters when trying to get a new project launched. Because I don't believe in reinventing the wheel, I met with various industry groups that offered meetings resources; I described the changing needs of corporate buyers, including procurement professionals who were increasingly being asked to help apply their expertise toward meetings purchasing and to assist with contract management.

You're probably familiar with the attitude that "meetings and events are very personal areas to manage." Or that "you can't tell planners they have to standardize sourcing and contracts because it's too decentralized." Actually, many of these same things were once said about corporate travel. It also became obvious that many meetings industry leaders considered contracts nothing but a necessary evil, although meetings contracts are probably one of the biggest risks for companies, given the millions spent yearly in cancellation and attrition fees.

What came from these realizations was a resolve to create—from scratch—a group of corporate travel/meeting experts who could put together educational materials to guide travel and procurement managers in this new, unchartered territory. I distinctly remember my meeting with the board, presenting my case findings and decision to create a new GBTA committee: the Groups and Meetings Committee. I thought long and hard about who was qualified to head up this new group, and I sought recommendations from industry colleagues. After a long and serious deliberation, I asked Tracy Wilt, manager of Global Travel and Meetings Management at Xerox, and Madlyn Caliri, who at the time was managing meetings for AT&T (she is now global procurement director at Reed Elsevier), to co-chair.

Under their leadership, the group quickly expanded to include many talented individuals, like Kari Kesler-Wendel, Rick Binford, Debi Scholar, and Mike Malinchok. In 2004, the committee coined the term *strategic meetings management* (SMM) and unveiled the first-ever SMM white paper, "Building a Strategic Meetings Management Program." A bounty of other papers and resources have followed since. My initial plan also included creating a session on SMM for the GBTA annual convention, where I was to step down and hand over the responsibility of the association to my successor, Carol Bailey, at the time the director of Corporate Travel for Burlington Northern & Santa Fe Railway Company.

Never did I ever think the group would go on to create a strategic meetings management program road map that would serve as the guiding foundation for organizations to learn about and develop their own SMMPs. The overriding success of the Groups and Meetings Committee spawned several task forces to create specific industry tools; these included the SMM Maturity Model (see Linda McNairy's chapter in this book) and the creation of a long-dreamed-of program of strategic meetings management certification (SMMC), a course of study designed for travel and procurement professionals.

The results of these efforts to establish SMM guidelines and resources are staggering. In today's $357 billion meetings market, it is estimated that 10%–25% savings can be achieved through the implementation of a robust SMMP, aided by state-of-the-art technology. Many programs boast even bigger returns. Success stories abound, and all the evidence points to the compelling value proposition of SMM.

This book focuses on the "art of the possible." The leading experts in the industry chronicle their foundational elements, describe current successes, and provide a glimpse into the future of SMM.

Looking back now, it all seems such a blur—from those first days of struggling to learn how to help travel and procurement managers, to the creation of a bank of sophisticated SMM resources and programs that are helping organizations of every size and in every region of the globe. It's been an amazing journey!

Like any other remarkable achievement, there were many individuals along the way who contributed to what is today *the* industry standard for strategically managing meetings and events: SMMP! This journey has been enhanced by the vision of some of my colleagues for whom I have the utmost respect. I want to thank all the accomplished industry thought leaders who have contributed to this book—for their expertise, their generosity, and valuable contributions to this industry! You have my deepest appreciation.

At first glance, the Global Business Travel Association (GBTA) Foundation's new strategic meetings management (SMM) Maturity Model might seem to only be for organizations that have adopted all aspects of a strategic meetings management program (SMMP) in a holistic approach. But the model—and its online Maturity Model Index tool, which enables companies to apply established measurements to assess their journey along their own SMM path—is just as suited to organizations just beginning to establish their SMMPs. The beauty of the model is that it helps meetings managers—regardless of what stage of SMM they are at—determine if and where there is room to grow in order to gain further savings and efficiencies. This chapter is written by Linda J. McNairy, vice president of Strategic Partner Management at StarCite, vice chair of GBTA's Groups and Meetings Committee, and a key figure in developing the model and index.

Maturing Your SMMP Program:
Getting to Where You Want to Be

by Linda J. McNairy

The great thing in the world is not so much where we stand, as in what direction we are moving.
— Oliver Wendell Holmes

This quote could not be a more appropriate way to describe the strategic objective of the SMM Maturity Model, created by the Global Business Travel Association Foundation in partnership with StarCite, Inc. Companies worldwide have adopted strategic meetings management programs to better manage a range of processes involved in planning their meetings and events: everything from budgeting, planning, sourcing, attendee management, payment, and analysis of business intelligence. A 2010 study by PhoCusWright, Inc. shows that 95% of US meeting managers have adopted at least some SMM modules enterprise–wide.

Some companies have only a few of the individual elements; some have a robust and overarching program. But regardless of the depth and reach of the individual elements, the incorporation of SMM components has been proven to provide value and opportunity

The SMM Maturity Model is inspired by a framework for process improvement created at Carnegie Mellon University as well as industry research, focus groups and white papers authored by the GBTA's Groups and Meetings Committee.

to the organizations' meetings and events activities. But the question remains: "How do I determine what is the right mix for my organization?"

The SMM Maturity Model and its online Maturity Model assessment tool enable companies to apply established measurements to evaluate their own SMM journey. (For more information, visit http://www.gbta.org.) The model helps them determine where there is room to grow and gain further savings and efficiencies. It is the responsibility of the SMM champion, whether they reside in travel, meetings, procurement, or elsewhere to decide whether to adopt a single element of SMM, embrace the entire system on a holistic basis, or improve upon what they've already integrated. After all, SMM champions know best their companies' own indirect expense management programs, as well as their readiness to advance their program. Any response to the assessment questions may be the "right answer" for any particular organization.

Why Do We Need a Model?

The SMM Maturity Model represents another natural outgrowth of the GBTA Groups and Meetings Committee's (GBTA GMC) ongoing and prolific work in the SMM space. Beginning with the 2004 creation of a white-paper series identifying best practices for an SMMP, the GBTA GMC set forth guidance on defining SMM, (*Strategic Meetings Management (SMM) is a disciplined approach to managing enterprise-wide meeting and event activities, processes, suppliers and data in order to achieve measurable business objectives that align with the organization's strategic goals/vision, and deliver value in the form of quantitative savings, risk mitigation and service quality.*) measuring meeting spend, analyzing opportunities, building the program framework, and then implementing systemwide. As part of its work, the organization also established the "Components of a Best-in-Class Strategic Meetings Management Program," which emphasizes how meetings management technology supports the holistic management of:

- Registration of meetings and events
- The approval process

- Sourcing and procurement
- Meeting planning and execution
- Payment and expense reconciliation
- Data analysis and reporting

Many companies have referred to this framework for envisioning the holistic representation of an SMMP. But the new Maturity Model provides a pathway to get there, a guide to assess where your company stands now, and recommendations on how and where to move forward.

The SMM Maturity Model Task Force[1] that created the Maturity Model felt strongly that SMMPs should work for all sizes and types of companies, not just global giants that have implemented many or all of the core elements of an SMMP enterprise–wide. And each SMMP should not be an exact duplication of all other SMMP implementations.

If a small or midsize company has adopted one or two elements, say, a managed e-sourcing program and automated attendee management, but not a unified system that includes a payment and reconciliation tool or data analysis and reporting, it doesn't mean they don't have a so-called "true" SMMP. And, more important, it doesn't mean they still can't track their progress and, if they wish, incorporate more SMMP elements over time and as needed for a fuller, more comprehensive program as timing becomes appropriate.

---

1 Task Force members included co-chairs Kari Kesler-Wendel, Sr., Director, Carlson Wagonlit Travel SMM Program Management & Solutions; Debi Scholar, President, Scholar Consulting Group; Linda J. McNairy, Vice President, Strategic Partner Management at StarCite Inc.; Carolyn Pund, Senior Global Meetings and Events Manager of Cisco Systems; Linda Bennitt, Director of Operations/Account Management at Maxvantage.

The Beauty of the Maturity Index

The main benchmarking feature of the SMM Maturity Model is the Maturity Model Index, an online tool residing on GBTA's website, which enables managers to assess where their companies stand in the SMMP process and where they can move forward to strengthen their programs. The index lists and rates various components that are part of SMM, included below:

- Strategy
- Policy
- Registration of events
- Approval
- Sourcing and procurement
- Supplier relationship management
- Payment and expense reconciliation
- Data analysis and reporting
- Meetings technology
- Stakeholder management (including training and development)
- Communication and leadership
- Measuring the three Rsp (return on objective, return on investment, and return on equity)
- Resource modeling and management

The tool enables SMMP champions to look at various stages of best practices for the processes mentioned above and determine where they are on a rating scale of 1 to 6.

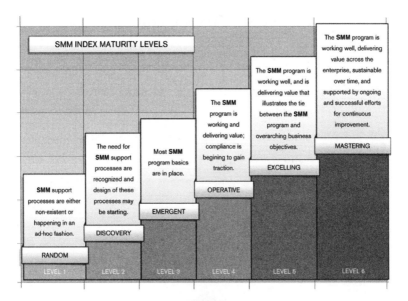

SMM INDEX MATURITY LEVELS

The SMM program is working well, delivering value across the enterprise, sustainable over time, and supported by ongoing and successful efforts for continuous improvement.

The SMM program is working well, and is delivering value that illustrates the tie between the SMM program and overarching business objectives.

The SMM program is working and delivering value; compliance is begining to gain traction.

Most SMM program basics are in place.

The need for SMM support processes are recognized and design of these processes may be starting.

SMM support processes are either non-existent or happening in an ad-hoc fashion.

MASTERING

EXCELLING

OPERATIVE

EMERGENT

DISCOVERY

RANDOM

LEVEL 1   LEVEL 2   LEVEL 3   LEVEL 4   LEVEL 5   LEVEL 6

For example, under the Maturity Model component "sourcing and procurement," in measuring the use and adoption of a preferred supplier program, an organization would score 1 (Random Meetings Management) if preferred suppliers are not in place for meetings and events. The score would be 2 if the company recognized the value of a preferred supplier program and put the basics in place, and a 3 would be earned if less than half of meetings and events adhere to preferred supplier programs in the business units where the SMMP was implemented.

Meanwhile, a score of 4 would mean that 50%–75% of meetings and events adhere to preferred supplier programs in implemented business units, while 5 would necessitate that 76%–90% of meetings and events adhere to preferred supplier programs for all meeting types and virtual meetings in business units implemented. At the top, mastery level 6, an organization has more than 91% of meetings and events adhering to preferred supplier programs enterprise–wide, according to the index.

Another important area of an SMMP is creating and communicating a meetings policy—governing everything from planning procedures to using preferred suppliers. In the area of communicating policy, on one end of the spectrum the index rates as 6 any organization that has set the SMM policy as the standard for how meetings and events are implemented. And all categories of the policy can be readily referenced—for example, via the corporate intranet—by any staff. Conversely, organizations that have not created a policy, and therefore have no need to communicate it, score a 1.

Take It Easy

While the SMM Maturity Model and Index enable companies to benchmark their progress against the mastery level of an SMMP, practitioners should also see the tools as a way to reassure themselves that where they are right now in their own program may be just the place they need to be. Rather than interpreting the tools as a point of reference showing where they "should" be on the SMMP scale (the tendency to immediately focus on the mastery level), it should provide SMM champions with the information they need to decide at what level they "want" to be, and how to get there.

There's no rush to creating the "perfect" SMMP. Indeed, it may be premature to push through a program just for the sake of having one, since your organization may not be properly prepared for the changes a systemwide SMMP would bring. However, the model enables you to get started as your organization prepares itself to manage a more mature program. Use the Maturity Model Index as a checklist to determine your pace so far and what needs to be done to advance. For example, in the area of "communication and leadership," are you at the point where SMM communication strategy and deployment is nonexistent? Or perhaps your communication strategy has been deployed across multiple stakeholder groups and the message content is customized for the audience.

Communication Strategy Progression

Mastering:
Multifaceted communication strategy and messaging deployed and successful across enterprise and with suppliers; communications are ongoing and messaging drives compliance.

Operative:
Communication strategy deployed across multiple stakeholder groups; the message content is customized for the audience.

Random:
SMM communication nonexistent, siloed or unknown.

But to advance to the mastery level, you'd need to implement a multifaceted communication strategy—across multiple stakeholders and business groups, and one that is woven into your firm's overall business strategy—and ongoing messaging across your entire enterprise, including and involving preferred suppliers. You'd also need to measure if those communications were pushing up levels of policy compliance. On the other hand, there may be other components of your SMMP program that need to be developed before you will want to be at mastery level in communications. The last thing you want to do is communicate and set expectations if your systems are not ready to support the usage.

The bottom line in working with the Maturity Model and its prescriptive report is to use them like an online road map, like www.mapquest.com. Once you enter your starting and destination points, you are presented with several alternatives for selecting your route: the shortest by distance, the roads that avoid major highways, the shortest by time, etc. You can select the route that is right for you, or even use a combination of several options. Use the new model's resources and information to support your program and plot desired advancement, rather than make it a measuring stick that will force you into creating something that doesn't fit your organization.

For many companies, creating and implementing a strategic meetings management program (SMMP) is a feat to be celebrated. But then there's that next step: expanding adoption of the program, a major challenge on its own. In this chapter, Mike Malinchok, who is a consultant and president of S2K Consulting, offers change management advice for getting that last, elusive 20% of your organization to participate in your program. Read this chapter to learn how to apply three tenets of change management to reach successful adoption: making your mission personal, making it matter, and making it simple.

Coaching Your Way to Full SMMP Adoption:
Getting the Holdouts in Your Company on Board

by Mike Malinchok

Coaching is about providing inspiration. Consulting is about providing information. Information plus inspiration equals performance acceleration.

— Jeremy Robinson

The Pareto principle, also known as the 80/20 rule, seems to have a derivation that applies to facilitating change within an organization. That is, change is an activity that requires 20% of your effort to accomplish the first 80% of the task and 80% of your effort for the last 20%. However, the value contained in that final 20% may well justify the entire effort. So when coaching that last 20% of employees to adopt your strategic meetings management program (SMMP), you'll need to vigorously employ some basic tenets of change management philosophy and strategies. The effort may be significant, but the results are worthwhile.

At many organizations, employees in highly visible and readily accessible pockets of business—the meetings department for example—can be relied upon to comply with new directives for their organizations' SMMPs. It is the last 20% or so of spend and meetings activities that takes place outside, across departments or divisions throughout the organization, that is typically elusive and requires a more deliberate change management strategy for capture.

This is where it is valuable to have both a universal meetings technology platform that makes it easier for employees to manage meetings, and executive coaching strategies to help deliver both the *information* and the *inspiration* to advance desired change.

Quite simply put, to most effectively coach your organization through that final hurdle to 100% adoption, the greatest return on your investment (ROI) of time and energy will be realized by emphasizing three of the basic tenets of change management:

1. Make it PERSONAL
2. Make it MATTER
3. Make it SIMPLE

This chapter will focus on the ways in which meetings, travel, and procurement managers, as well as other practitioners, can apply these three tenets of change management to create an optimal environment in order to reach successful levels of SMMP adoption— whether that is the final 20% of targeted volume or simply a 20% increase of current volume.

Making It PERSONAL

The most important first step is to actually define what you consider successful SMMP adoption levels. If there is missing spend volume that you want to capture, start by developing a clearly articulated vision of what that is. That means identifying the budget holders and focusing on the exact programs where there are deviations to policy. In this stage, making it personal should leave you with no doubt as to where your efforts are aimed.

Because this step is so specific and personal, special care and attention must be placed on the emotional and political sensitivities that could be in play when approaching these stakeholders. Understanding why these spend pockets have been elusive will be just as important as identifying the value they will bring to the program.

It is also important to understand the specific work processes that individuals are utilizing when planning meetings. Meeting planning is not likely to be the primary focus of these individuals' jobs. It may be a major headache they're faced with on top of their primary responsibilities. It may also be a "perk" that provides the employee with opportunities to travel or get away from his or her day-to-day tasks. Understanding these motivations helps frame the discussion for describing the benefits from an SMMP or the use of meetings technology to streamline time-consuming tasks, such as procuring hotels or marketing events with online registration sites. Providing a standardized "contracts and approval" process may also relieve major areas of stress for employees who may have, on their own, been treading on uncertain territory.

More than at any other time in your program's evolution, this is when you need to be exceptionally versed and accurate in your facts, as there is a low margin for error in this stage. Theoretical hypotheses or best-practice estimations are not going to give you the kind of clout you'll need to attain full adoption.

Given that you have roughly 80% of activity incorporated into your SMMP, that success means that you are now in a position to speak from a place of organizational authority as to what your company aims to accomplish by full participation in an SMMP. In addition, to back up your assessment of nonparticipation, you are more than likely in a very strategically powerful position with your supplier partners, for example, preferred hotels, to pull actual data from them on any leakage in spend that is not coming through your program.

So, be bold—be specific—and BE PERSONAL.

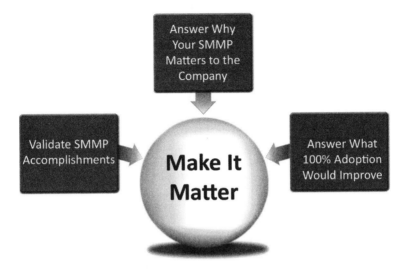

Making It MATTER

In order to make your desired adoption level matter or, to put it another way, make adoption of your SMMP a meaningful goal to employees, it helps to be able to objectively and cohesively draw a direct correlation between the benefits of the SMMP and the company's ability to achieve its corporate mission. If you are not able to articulate that correlation, you are missing a critical communication component that enables you to effectively drive change by *making it* MATTER.

One way to make your SMMP matter to employees is to demonstrate your program's validated accomplishments over the past twelve-month period. Make a list of the objective, measured, and validated accomplishments; they should be unambiguous and leave no room for interpretation. Next, look at your company's high-level mission statement or goals directive. Consider what it is that your company does for the market it serves or for the world at large.

There's no minimizing the importance of this step. You must be able to answer the question "Why does the SMMP matter to our company?" To help you determine why your SMMP matters, fill in the blanks in this simple connect-the-dots exercise below:

With the benefits that the SMMP provides, such as _____, our company is able to _____, enabling us to _____. Thus our SMMP contributes directly to our company's mission of_____.

This exercise is something you might very well have done in the early stages of your SMMP as a way of gaining initial stakeholder adoption. So, while this may be repetitive, it truly is a message that can never be overstated.

Additionally, as you seek to capture that final 20% of meetings and event activity that you don't now have, you need to answer this question: "What would 100% of our company's SMMP potential adoption allow for, enable, or make possible that is not possible today at our current level of adoption?" As before, the answer must be irrefutable, fact based, objective, and specific or else it simply won't MATTER enough to carry you through the pains of change.

SMMP ADOPTION Change Analysis	PAIN	GAIN
CURRENT STATE (status quo)	1. What is *missing* from my current process of managing meetings/events? How am I adversely impacted?	2. How is my current process of managing meetings/events working well for me? What key value is it providing to me?
FUTURE STATE (fold into the SMMP)	3. What *costs* have to be paid in order to make the change? What do I have to *give up* by adopting the SMMP?	4. What are the benefits to me in moving my meetings into the SMMP? *What is in it for me?*

Making it SIMPLE

One of the most powerful change management techniques employed in executive coaching is an exercise known as the Pain/Gain Model. It helps to clarify decision making into as much of a no-brainer process as possible. Each scenario needs to be identified, validated, and then measured in order to make the decision to change a simple one.

For true sustainable change, the highest odds for success are present when the following are in place:

1. Future-state gains are of more value than current-state gains.
2. Future-state pains are acceptable investments (of time, money, or energy), which are more palatable than current-state pains.

Technology Makes It Simple

This is where some of the benefits of meetings technology really factor into the picture. Meetings technology, which is a major component in an SMMP, provides employees with preconfigured forms and tools to manage their meetings. Show them the benefits of utilizing a standardized request for proposal (RFP) and centralized supplier database for sourcing, versus having to surf a million websites or call suppliers one by one. Let them see the online registration tools that can utilize corporate templates that allow someone to create a professional-looking registration website without having to use online programming code.

The benefits of meetings technology are very compelling. Planning a meeting can be one of the most detail-oriented, time-consuming projects. In addition, if meetings or events are client facing, involving company executives, the spotlight will be on how well the planner did his or her job.

Conclusion: Inspiration Drives Change

Successful change management happens most often when the individual who is required to make the behavioral shift is engaged and inspired to do so.

You are on your way to success with those individuals who have control over that final 20% of meeting spend:

If you have made the change PERSONAL, then they are thinking, "I'm vested in listening to what you're asking."

If you have made the change MATTER, then they are expressing, "I want to do a good job and be a good corporate citizen, and this makes sense to me."

If you have made it SIMPLE, then they are showing you that "You understand me and have made this a low-risk decision on my part. I respect you and am grateful for that."

As top executive coach David L. Dotlich has said, "Coaching is a process that fosters self-awareness and that results in the motivation to change, as well as the guidance needed if change is to take place in ways that meet organizational needs."

As your strategic meetings management program (SMMP) matures through the years, what should your expectations be for long-term savings? This chapter by George Odom, president of the consulting firm, Strategic Travel & Meetings Group, walks you through all the key phases of an SMMP—from Program Justification (putting together a business plan, collecting spend data, and getting senior management to be your "advocate"), to "Improvement and Understanding" (trending with historical data, improving service, and reducing budgets with saving, to "Strategic Management and Long-term Success" (policies are in place, examining supplier agreements, and looking for improvements), to "Maturity" (instituted a formal Supplier Relationship Program to foster closer cooperation with vendors and the opportunities to achieve incremental savings yearly are greatly diminished; service levels are high and costs are under control). This is the strategic how-to manual for building successful meetings programs and supplier relationships!

Continuous Improvement of SMMPs: Knowing You Have Arrived

by George Odom

The ultimate long-term goal for your SMMP should be to achieve zero savings!

That statement is an exaggeration for effect. Moreover, zero savings flies in the face of what an SMMP is largely all about: saving money and avoiding costs as well as reducing process costs for everything from planning to attendee management.

It should more correctly be said that your goal should be to grow and enhance your SMMP through various stages of development, all the while identifying and reaping savings, fine-tuning strategy, deepening relationships with suppliers, and improving service levels. And, at some point in the life of your program, when it has matured, you'll get to a point of diminishing *year-over-year* or *incremental* savings. That's when you know you have arrived—you are a success.

Why Create an SMMP?

It is a big leap getting to that stage of success, however. First you have to navigate and achieve several phases of SMMP development, including creating and justifying your program, improving and understanding it, and achieving long-term success.

Let's begin by examining three overarching reasons for creating your SMMP:

- Service
- Savings
- Continuous improvement

Service, of course, has to be the largest focus. If users—however you may characterize them, whether they are planners, attendees or both—do not have their meeting objectives met, there is not much chance of achieving savings opportunities. If meeting support isn't there, or it fails, it will not matter how much you have saved or how little things cost.

Once you have achieved and implemented the correct level of service, it is important to not become complacent. You should always strive for improvement. This can be done by offering better services, aggressively managing budgets, creating preferred supplier agreements, and purchasing goods and services at the best price.

• Maturity
• Zero Savings

Phase IV

Phase III

• Strategic Management
• Long-term Success

• Program Improvement
• Program Understanding
  (among stakeholders)

Phase II

Phase I

• Creation of Program
• Program Justification

The overall objective should not be buying things cheaply or at the absolute lowest possible price. Rather, it should be buying the right things at the right price. The price should be fair for the buyer as well as the purchaser, creating a win-win relationship. Many SMMP programs are tasked with achieving savings, but as an SMMP matures the ultimate goal should in fact be to have reached a level of efficiency that allows for a rich, robust meetings program, having already captured the incremental savings, that is, "zero savings."Before this idea is explored in more depth, it is important to look at the phases an SMMP will go through.

- Phase I: Beginning and Program Justification
- Phase II: Improvement and Understanding
- Phase III: Strategic Management and Long-term Success
- Phase IV: Maturity and Zero Savings

A quick look at the different phases:

Phase I:
Beginning and Program Justification

After you have done your due diligence and put together an SMMP business case, you are then tasked with getting your program up and running. There is a variety of data[2] and guesstimates on how much money can be saved as well as how much it will cost to actually run the program.

---

2 StarCite benchmarking data shows companies can save up to 25% of meetings costs by implementing SMMP technology.

At this phase the objective is to capture everything you can to justify your existence and your program. You should strive to capture and communicate any type of cost savings, any type of cost avoidance, time savings, or risk mitigation you can claim. The chance to show value is paramount, especially when some of your internal customers are not sure they want you to succeed. There will be vocal opponents who will try to find fault and create reasons for your program to fail, or at least try to show they can run their meetings better than you can. This should be expected. At this stage, remember to put 80% of your effort into the 80% of your customers who want your help and assistance. You'll address those who want to throw stones at your program during the next phase.

Data is king during Phase I. For example, it is crucial to capture such things as what cities your meetings are being held in. Other important information: What hotels you are using? What time of year are you meeting most? Who are your biggest internal customers—Sales and Marketing, HR, Information Technology? Why are they having meetings? What is important to them? What can you do better to help them meet their objectives? What is the amount of their budgets versus the actual cost of the meeting? When people give you feedback, are you capturing it, finding a solution, and then communicating back to them that you have heard them and made changes?

This is a time when management needs to understand your successes and your challenges. Senior management can be your advocate if you are honest and balanced in your reporting. In this phase, you are developing your savings methodology.

Since you don't have preferred programs yet in place and you really don't have historical data to use to determine that you are buying smarter, savings is usually based off a standard or benchmark. To determine how well they are purchasing, most companies use "first quote" as the baseline. This is compared to what was actually purchased after negotiations. And the difference is the savings. During Phase I, you can also capture savings for items you do not have to purchase, i.e., cost avoidance. This can include an upgraded break or an offer of free welcoming beverages when you were not planning on offering them.

The amount of savings as a percentage of your managed spend that you are able to achieve during Phase I will be the largest amount you will have during the life of your program.

Phase II:
Improvement and Understanding

In Phase II, you will have started to gather actual historical data and are now using the information to look at trends. You have put service standards into place and are evaluating suppliers. You are looking to continue to improve and to increase your services, and your internal customers see you as a service that has enabled them to focus on their core competencies.

You are not perceived as a threat but more as a partner. Yes, there are still pockets of resistance, but these are becoming smaller and less frequent. You have many success stories, many of them coming from your internal customers.

At this stage, savings methodologies are usually reexamined. Many companies now look at the definition of savings as the amount of money that can be taken out of a budget. Said another way, when your internal customers' budgets were set, they didn't know you were going to be able to negotiate some services that would enable them to have the meeting or event they had planned at less expense than they had budgeted. The expectation is now that you will achieve that same type of savings in future years. So next year's budgets can be reduced based on the reductions realized in the present year. The savings will still be there, but they become less obvious.

Cost avoidance is looked at as a nice benefit and a success, but the real measure of success is the savings based on hard savings that can be removed from a budget. Management has started to recognize the successes of the SMMP and is requesting information on how the program compares to the marketplace, and they want industry benchmarks. The amount of data you are collecting is growing; you now look at the data less as how well you have done but more as what future opportunities for cost savings and supplier leverage are available.

Phase III:
Strategic Management and Long-term Success

In Phase III you have become adept at mining your data. You have systems in place to monitor and proactively manage your SMMP. You have become a partner to your internal customers and they can't see conducting an event or meeting without the program's assistance. You are asked for data to help internal customers budget for the next year. You are seen as a resource, and management values your opinion and knowledge. This is a good place to be!

Policies are in place and controls and audits are done to confirm compliance. You are able to truly show how the SMMP benefits the corporation. During this phase you are looking even more critically at your suppliers. Not all the suppliers you started your program with are still part of your program. Those that have progressed with you understand your program, your internal customers, and your needs and requirements.

In this phase, you are looking at long-term supplier partnerships and examining negotiated agreements with them: hotels, meeting-planning organizations, technology providers, as well as support and ancillary services. You are measuring the success of these agreements with service-level agreements (SLAs) that spell out what activities and services are required.

There may be financial compensation for your company if the service levels are not met, but the goal is not to require penalty payments from your business partners. Rather it is to ensure that services are supplied at the levels required. At this phase, you understand how suppliers price their services. If suppliers offer you bundled pricing, you know the individual elements that go into that package. You have a good feel for salaries, overhead, and profits.

In Phase III you are looking for constant improvement and strategic thinking is routine. You continue to be measured on the amount of hard-dollar savings by upper management, but because you have successfully negotiated agreements that may be three to five years in length, and because you have already built significant levels of savings into your budgets, the incremental amount of savings achieved annually is likely to be less readily obvious. But in actuality, it is compounding and continues to grow. You may now hold supplier meetings and reviews where you are more concerned about what can be done to increase services and savings in the future and less on negotiating costs.

Some of your suppliers thrive in this type of environment, while others see it as always being asked to do more but not being able to charge more. Data is king in this phase also. Numbers are used to build business cases, show service advancement, customer response, and satisfaction as well as savings.

Phase IV:
Maturity and Zero Savings

Phase IV is the level you have been working toward since you started the SMMP program. You have total understanding of how your program supports the corporate goals and objectives. You understand your internal customer groups, and you are an integral part of their programs. You are able to show true value to them. They see the SMMP group as giving them an advantage over their competition.

Here, too, there is true integration between suppliers and your corporation. The corporation looks to the suppliers you have selected as best-in-class and innovators. You have been able to negotiate long-term agreements and have won preferred pricing agreements with the lowest rates possible. You have selected the best suppliers and they are committed to bringing continued value to your company and to the SMMP program.

You see the difference between tactical suppliers and strategic suppliers. The strategic suppliers are more important. If you had to change one of these suppliers, it would be much more difficult and disruptive to service, internal departments, and the company. These are the suppliers you spend your time and effort with.

In this phase, the supplier/buyer differentiation becomes blurred.

> Under an SRM program, you meet with strategic suppliers to manage service-level agreements (SLAs). Schedule meetings with agendas and set deliverables. Expect suppliers to come with data and an understanding of the program.

The suppliers see their mission as bringing the best outcomes to your company and consistently bring ideas and suggestions for improvements. You have instituted a formal and thorough Supplier Relationship Management (SRM) program and have determined how each supplier's services impact your company.

When conducting such meetings with suppliers, expect them to come in with data and an understanding of the program. This is the time to review past performance; look at what had been agreed upon to do since the last meeting; discuss if those goals were met and then talk about what will be done in the future. The person serving as the suppliers' advocate within the organization needs to understand their business, their opportunities, and their challenges in order to better understand how to best service the company. It should be a mutually beneficial relationship. And through SRM, the organization can leverage the suppliers' expertise, keep service levels high and costs under control.

Because the organization understands the suppliers' pricing structures, the agreements are fair for both parties. Since various suppliers have been analyzed, there is assurance that the best partners have been chosen for the corporation's program. You have reached long-term agreements such that the year-to-year savings are small. In fact, your goal in Phase IV is to strive for zero incremental savings. You might look at it this way: the smaller the growth in your year-over-year savings are in this phase, the more successful you are.

This is not to say that the company is paying high prices or is not cost or service conscious. It is in fact just the opposite, because you have already driven all possible excessive costs out of the optimized program. Because you understand your data, the service requirements, and the marketplace, and since you have put long-term agreements in place with the best suppliers, the opportunity to achieve additional new savings every year is diminished, although the accumulated savings are dramatic.

So you have a meetings management program in place but senior management does not mandate that your planners abide by official policy or even use preferred vendors. Operating this way, how do you make your SMMP as effective as possible and produce maximum savings and control? Before joining StarCite, Louann Cashill, manager of Strategic Projects, managed a nonmandated meetings services program at Toyota Motor Sales U.S.A. In this chapter, she offers guidance about how to get your SMMP noticed by key stakeholders and senior management. Cashill advises on getting buy-in from key parties, partnering with suppliers, and measuring important statistics such as cost savings and cost avoidance to gain solid return on investment (ROI) figures. The goal is to expand your program as much as possible, maximize savings, and control and elevate risk mitigation—even if you have no official recognition, or mandate, from above.

SMMP Success— Without a Mandate

by Louann Cashill

Anyone who has successfully introduced and furthered change within their organization will tell you that it's an act of bravery. What's more, convincing executives and other stakeholders to get behind you on new initiatives can often be downright frightening! However, these changemakers will also likely tell you that it was one of the most rewarding career moves they have ever undertaken. This chapter is dedicated to the fearless travel, procurement, or meetings professional who is willing to drive a few stakes into the ground in order to introduce change and create strategy for meetings management.

No Mandate? No Problem

Is formal, executive support at your organization a work in progress? Perhaps it's tentative? Or worse, maybe your senior executives are hesitant to throw their support behind your strategic meetings management program (SMMP) initiatives?

The reality is that few organizations have much, if any, focus on meetings, incentives, or tradeshows because these events are typically budgeted across individual departments, divisions, business units, and practice groups. Capturing data on meetings spend and volume, individual attendee information, spend, volume, and ROI, regardless how significant it may be, is typically not a core business objective and is often considered somewhat irrelevant. Organizations subject to government regulations, such as public companies or those within certain industries such as financial services and healthcare[3] are the exception but, unfortunately, not the rule.

Bringing attention to meetings, becoming more visible to stakeholders and executives, and gaining strong support for an SMMP can be a full-time job in itself. However, it is encouraging to know that you can, and should, move forward toward elevating your meetings initiatives through effective strategy. Approval and support from *every* executive and business unit is unlikely and would actually be somewhat unusual. The stakeholders who most need to understand and get behind the benefits and opportunities for efficiency are the ones who actually sponsor, pay for, and make decisions impacting your organization's meetings, incentives, and tradeshows.

---

3 For example, for healthcare companies, the Physician Payments Sunshine Provisions of the Patient Protection and Affordable Care Act of 2009.

Raising Awareness of Your SMMP

Data is the holy grail in creating an overall awareness of your SMMP. Among other key criteria, credible data will support a framework for the components of an SMMP that offer the most immediate opportunities.

Numerous articles, white papers, webcasts, and workshops are available on the subject of data collection. They offer guidance on what to collect, where it might reside, what it can be used for, and how to analyze it. Your primary goal in the beginning is to gather the data to illustrate a story and provide a compelling business case for adopting your strategic meetings strategy. Keep in mind, however, that your organization is unique. What may be important to demonstrate to one organization, or to one leadership contingent, may be relatively unimportant for another. In any event, the research will nearly always uncover some interesting and useful results. Key findings might come from: (see next page)

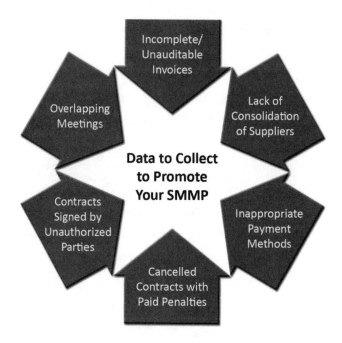

- Cancelled hotel contracts that involve paid damages
- Contracts and agreements signed by unauthorized signers or third parties on the company's behalf
- Overlapping meetings held in the same location during the same time frame
- Invoices that are not auditable and lack supporting documentation
- Lack of consolidation of meetings suppliers used across business units
- Meetings paid for with personal credit cards or department purchasing cards

The list is endless. But so is your opportunity to leverage your findings and build the foundation of your business case. Remember, your goal is not to embarrass any of your colleagues, but only to bring some visibility to meeting activity that is currently unmanaged. At times, you may believe that your organization's approach to meetings may even resemble the "Wild, Wild West" and the strategy at hand is far too enormous and intimidating.

There are many tools you can use to further your goals. For example, generally, people enjoy giving their opinion about things, and a well-developed survey can solve some mysteries around your organization's meetings. A survey can also create awareness and prepare the organization for an upcoming change. Develop surveys that contain questions with numerical values for responses, which can then be ranked. Also important is to encourage feedback by providing areas for comment. Surveys are extremely useful in determining who your company's occasional planners are, the volume and type of events they plan, their individual and (most important) collective spend on meetings, and existing processes for decision making. Most important, surveys can provide the opportunity to benchmark progress.

To "Policy" or Not to "Policy"

A formal meetings policy is not always the path of least resistance in operating an effective meetings program. Most of us who have spent time in mid- to large-size organizations are painfully aware that policies are not always followed and oftentimes there exists a complacent approach to compliance.

Without a policy or mandate stemming straight from the top, you are left to your own devices to gain adoption and expansion. This is when the ability to convert obstacles into opportunities will enable you to realize the flexibility that you actually have in this situation. You are not held to a written set of rules at this point and don't have to gain approvals when an element of the "policy" needs to be changed.

A policy can be threatening, particularly when it comes to meetings. Stakeholders and others can become extraordinarily territorial as they cling to the "tried and true" method of doing things, their relationships and loyalty to suppliers, their delight with site inspections, and an overall resistance to change. In the absence of a formal, written policy, your approach can seem far less invasive. In fact, an SMMP is designed to solve challenges, not *create* them. You are empowered to approach your audience on the basis of service, risk management, cost savings, and organizational efficiencies versus control.

However, if your organization does have a policy, it is important to have consistent processes in place for compliance; for example, defined consequences and an established approval system. Otherwise, consider the policy only "suggested guidelines." If you do not have a policy in place, do not be discouraged from eventually creating one. The bottom line is that a formal, written policy is a strategy that makes fundamental common sense.

Master the Art of Being Adaptive

All organizations have "cultures" or "identities" and no two are exactly alike. Not understanding your organization—all of it—can cost your initiatives both time (resulting from setbacks) and credibility. If you are new to the organization, the need to adapt and learn quickly will become instrumental to success, both with implementing an SMMP and to your career with the company in general. Look for a mentor in this area; not necessarily your direct manager but someone who has been successful within your organization on many fronts.

Engaging Appropriate Stakeholders from the Start

An important step in building a consolidated meetings strategy that is commonly overlooked is a failure to align all the appropriate stakeholders at the beginning of the process. You'll become painfully aware of it if you have failed to include a key contingent, whether you are developing a formal policy or not. Significant delays and setbacks are often the result of a person or group of people whose input was not sought out and represented. When you conduct due diligence in identifying the appropriate people (or their designated proxy), you save yourself from redundant work, frustration, delays, and unintended consequences later on.

Some ideas for assembling the "guest list" include forming a task force, conducting a focus group or surveys, speaking and meeting with a variety of potentials, and asking the simple question "Who else would you recommend I include?"

Develop Partnerships with Key Suppliers

The degree of influence that key suppliers have throughout your organization can be significant. In some environments, key suppliers have been business partners for quite some time and have gained the visibility and confidence of colleagues, executives, and entire work groups.

Get your preferred business partners engaged early in the implementation of your SMMP. Spend some time educating them on your priorities, challenges, goals, and areas you believe might be opportunities for them through various stages of your SMMP. Then allow them to share the same with you about their business, products, and services. Far too frequently, there is the sense that one party has to lose if the other party is to win. How untrue! Genuine partnerships that endure and even mature and evolve are ones that create a sense of "winning" across the entire enterprise of suppliers, creating high-performing, motivated work groups.

Metrics That Matter

Some key measurements that will help you gain visibility, credibility, and confidence among meetings stakeholders and executives relate directly back to the success of your hotel-sourcing program. They will also identify the very trends that enable forecasting versus reacting. They are:

Metrics That Matter

Cost Savings

- Sleeping rooms
- Meeting room rental
- Negotiated concessions; for example, comps, amenities, upgrades
- Reused attrition or cancellation fees paid

Cost Avoidance

- Food and beverage minimums
- Negotiated rebook clauses
- Negotiated attrition clauses
- Negotiated cancellation clauses

Credibility in this area is critical. A reliable data source, consistent definitions, and sound methodology for key performance indicators will ensure that, on the day you are presenting to your executives, you will do so with complete confidence and conviction.

Once you have historical data (at least six months to a year), it can be used to forecast future meetings spend. During annual budget-planning time, the data can bring insight and credibility to the process. Support the appropriate stakeholders by providing them with key data such as:

- Estimated meeting spend based on objectives
- Estimated meeting volume and attendance
- Opportunities to combine meetings and reduce overlapping or redundant meetings
- Best practices to reduce the cost of the stakeholder's meetings (e.g., using second-tier cities, being flexible in dates or location, and using preferred suppliers)

This is the type of initiative that demonstrates alignment and relevance to stakeholders and executives. Become a proven problem solver within your organization.

Effectively Communicating to Stakeholders

The art of communication can be thought of as an exchange of information between individuals and the presence of a sense of *mutual* understanding. An effective communication strategy will, to a large extent, determine the ultimate growth and success of your organization's meetings management initiatives. A failure to plan in this area is, most certainly, a plan to fail.

Ensure that your communications deliver a consistent and compelling message that speak to the listening audience. A message you have predetermined will support you in achieving your highest goals and objectives.

Conduct focus groups to gather information from current or potential stakeholders. That information may be used to change strategies, if necessary, to more closely align with your target audience's objectives. Focus groups can be held face-to-face or via webcast. The key is to gather a significant sampling so that results are not skewed. A focus group's opinions, perceptions, views, experiences, beliefs, and attitudes can all be used to improve and grow your strategic meetings initiatives.

Stakeholder groups' interests and concerns are usually varied. Presentations to them should be customized to speak to what is important to each and should also demonstrate how your strategy benefits them. Some stakeholder groups to note:

- Finance and Procurement: Their primary focus is typically on concepts such as how meetings impact the bottom line, meetings spend data across the enterprise, approvals, payment processes, opportunities to reduce costs, and supplier contracting.

- Marketing: Your marketing group is motivated to use meetings and events to enhance brand awareness and key messaging and to expand market penetration.

- Sales: The Sales group typically relies on meetings, incentives, and tradeshows to develop and strengthen relationships with existing or potential customers, motivate sales team members, and grow sales. This group may be most interested in how to more effectively use meetings, incentives, and tradeshows to increase sales and customer satisfaction.

- Training: This department conducts meetings, workshops, seminars, and courses where the focus is on education or experiential learning to improve skills and behaviors. It is not unusual for Training meetings to operate with small budgets. In addition, it is not unusual for Training (or a subset of the group) to support sales objectives. Demonstrating the benefits of leveraging the organization's buying power with suppliers, efficiency gains through consistent and automated processes, industry best practices, and best-in-class examples and logistical streamlining through an SMMP will maximize your support from—and credibility with—this group.

Maintaining the Big Picture

Throughout your campaign, keep your perspective broad and think strategically. Rather than focusing on the tactical aspects of meetings, your attention should be directed to the big picture, communicating the benefits of incorporating an SMMP into your organization, and developing a program that supports the organization's key business objectives.

Some successful approaches to communicating SMMP initiatives include webinars for various internal audiences within the organization. These can be relatively easy and inexpensive to produce and record for replays. You could also include a live question-and-answer component at the end to address questions and personalize the experience. Lunch and Learns, postings on the landing page of your company's intranet (for example, posting cancelled hotel space available for reuse), your own department's web page (a great place for testimonials), and presentations at other departmental meetings that have a stake in meetings (bring food!). Again, occasional surveys of stakeholders can serve a variety of purposes. Summarize the data and feedback afterward, which you can use to get in front of key stakeholders and executives.

Town halls or all-company meetings are also a great opportunity to request some type of "honorary mention" by executives or highlight the results of measuring the ROI of your meetings strategy. Don't miss an opportunity to post wins and positive metrics on your intranet. Allow your best assets and achievements to do the heavy lifting for you by posting testimonials from satisfied clients who have benefited from your strategic meetings initiatives.

Success Is Possible!

Even in a decentralized and nonmandated environment, you have powerful tools to demonstrate the value of your SMMP and to expand its influence across your organization. Leverage best practices, industry expertise, knowledge of your buying power with suppliers, and every educational resource available to continuously refine the blueprint for growth of your SMMP.

You can achieve success by educating your organization on meetings, reaching out to your colleagues throughout the industry for best practices, and keeping a positive attitude. Keep your focus on the target, think strategically, engage and invite stakeholders into the process and consistently evaluate and improve!

We live in an unsafe, unpredictable world of social media-driven revolutions, erupting volcanoes, earthquakes, tsunamis, and other horrors. As a result, risk mitigation for meetings is becoming more of a hot topic everywhere. Meetings managers need to be prepared not only to protect their company's financial interest and brand but also to be ready, at a moment's notice, to rescue meetings attendees stranded by natural disasters and political upheavals. In this chapter, UK-based specialist business travel writer Amon Cohen explores Europe's special meetings risk factors and makes a strong case for meetings managers globally to develop risk management plans in their SMMPs.

Risk Management and Meetings: The View from EMEA

by Amon Cohen

Stories abound about our newly risk-averse Western culture. However, on a professional level, for meetings managers, this is nothing but good news. Risk is not their enemy but their friend.

Here's why. Corporations are becoming increasingly obsessed with risk management, almost to the point where executive boards are as concerned with mitigating risk as they are with generating profits. It has become a big industry, with ratings agencies assessing companies' risk management strategies as part of their evaluations and corporations setting up stand-alone risk departments. In addition, legislation is getting tougher, such as the UK's Corporate Manslaughter and Corporate Homicide Act, and individuals are becoming more litigious.

In consequence, risk management provides a cast-iron reason for companies to have a strategic meetings management program (SMMP) along with a trained and experienced meetings expert to run it. There are numerous ways in which risk applies to corporate meetings, and it will quickly become apparent that the range of these risks touches many different corporate functions, including travel, human resources, legal, finance, security, and even corporate communications. Unless there is a central meetings department and established processes and procedures to centralize planning and sourcing for events, it will be almost impossible to track and coordinate management of meetings in a coherent fashion. Since the essence of risk management is the systematic assessment and mitigation of risk, your company needs an SMMP to ensure this happens for its meetings.

As with so many corporate processes, little rocket science is required (one exception: value-added tax; see below). Instead, awareness and willingness from the meetings manager and senior management to tackle the challenge on a sustained basis will win most of the battle.

Creating a Strategy

Some valuable intelligence exists that offers guidance on how to build good risk management programs. One industry white paper by Advito ('C'est la vie?': A Step-by-Step Guide to Building a Travel Risk Management Program," Advito, February 2009), written primarily in respect to transient, or individual, business travel advocates a six-step process:

1. Assign management responsibility: who is going to manage and sponsor your risk strategy?
2. Determine risk types: create a matrix of risk types specific to your organization.
3. Assess risk exposure: plot your organization's exposure to those specific threats.
4. Mitigate or manage: use tools for traveler tracking, creating information (policy and training), planning (crisis management), and risk transfer (providing insurance and medical assistance).

5. Communicate: make meetings participants aware of the program and their responsibilities.

6. Audit: monitor the program and adapt it to the constantly changing risk environment.

The Advito report also reproduces a very useful risk maturity model from an earlier paper by the Global Business Travel Association/iJET that will help you assess how good your organization is at travel risk management and how it can improve.

There is another useful model to remember for this subject: the four Ts of risk mitigation. Once a risk has been identified, there are four ways to mitigate it:

- Treat: exert internal controls to reduce the risk.
- Transfer: persuade or pay a third party to take the risk, e.g. buy insurance.
- Terminate: abort the activity.
- Tolerate: take no action because there are no viable options or the cost is disproportionate.

For further reading on developing and deploying risk mitigation strategies, especially in the meetings arena, please refer to"Bridging the Gap: Mitigating Meetings Risk,"[5] a StarCite white paper.

5 Access at http://www2.starcite.com/starcite/resourcecenter/downloads/StarCite-Meetings-Risk-Management.

Risks Applying to Meetings

The following list is neither complete nor authoritative, but should provide some pointers and illustrate the diversity of risks relating to meetings. The remarks are directed at risk issues in Europe in particular, although many apply globally.

Security

Management of the security of transient travelers has improved dramatically since 9/11. There are well-developed tracking tools, based on reservations made in global distribution systems; a good flow of destination advisories to travelers; and many corporations now have coherent crisis management plans for providing assistance and, if necessary, emergency repatriation.

For meetings, the picture is less clear. In general, companies seem to adopt security processes and systems with transient travelers primarily in mind and give little thought to whether they are relevant to meetings delegates as well. For example, most tracking systems are only helpful if the meetings participant has booked his or her travel through a preferred intermediary, such as a retained travel management company. But, for domestically staged conferences in particular, the delegate often elects to drive, or books a flight or rail ticket independently.

Luckily, the 2010 ash cloud crisis created an emergency where many travelers were inconvenienced without being at physical risk. As a result, it was an excellent opportunity to review security measures once more. One of the main lessons was that mobile technology is changing the game. On the downside, mobile phones and other tools are helping employees to make independent (and often unwise) decisions about how to overcome travel disruptions. On the upside, mobile is now emerging as a fast way to interact and assist with all employees regardless of how they got to where they are.

Meetings technology is also very helpful for delegate tracking. An electronic pre-event registration process will provide an accurate list of who is supposed to be attending an event. The registration process can also be utilized to collect travel and contact information for delegates, especially via end-to-end meetings technology systems that planners and managers can use to access data at a moment's notice.

While policies and systems are not always compatible with the needs of a meeting, the reverse is also true: meetings organizers need to check that their decisions do not risk contravening established security procedures. Take the case of booking a conference in a destination with relatively few air connections, say Dubrovnik, Croatia. The chances of numerous employees from the same organization being on the same flight are much higher than usual, and that could breach policies about the maximum number permitted on one aircraft for business continuity reasons.

At the very least, it is important to create a crisis management plan for any large meeting, laying out sensible contingencies for making a group safe, including, if necessary, getting people home quickly. There also needs to be contingency planning in case of cancellation before an event has even started. In such cases, balanced risk assessment is necessary. There are risks in being overcautious about cancelling events, too, such as pulling a conference in Paris because terrorists have detonated a bomb on the other side of Europe in

Istanbul. Premature cancellations can not only be expensive but can also damage goodwill among everyone from delegates to suppliers.

Health and Safety

The influential UK Corporate Manslaughter and Homicide Act of 2007 changed attitudes toward duty of care worldwide. It helped reinforce a presumption that all companies should make systemic assessments of health and safety risks, and it also made clear that the workplace (and therefore liability for employee welfare) is not restricted to regular company locations.

As a result, an employee at a conference is in a workplace and it is therefore important to carry out health and safety assessments of the meeting venue. The UK's Institute of Travel & Meetings (ITM) publishes a comprehensive sample venue assessment form in a white paper on its website entitled "Procuring Meetings & Events: Part 1: The Groundwork" (accessible with ITM membership).

The ITM form, running to dozens of pages, covers everything from fire certification to electrical wiring to food allergies and illustrates how endemic box-ticking risk aversion has become. Similar assessments are required for other suppliers, such as audio-visual providers. That makes another good argument for having an SMMP: if your company has created a preferred meetings supplier program, you only have to vet the list once in a while, not on a meeting-by-meeting basis. However, do remember that any unusual activities, especially involving anything or anyone that moves, will require additional assessment.

One last tip: the biggest and most overlooked employee health and safety risk is driving a car. If you have delegates driving to a conference, consider creating rules, such as maximum mileage in a day, which will limit their exposure to risk.

Financial Compliance

In the European Union (EU), the biggest challenge to meetings-related financial risk is value-added tax (VAT) rules, which are horrendously complicated when it comes to meetings. As an unintended consequence of a complex mechanism called the Tour Operators' Margin Scheme (originally designed to avoid VAT liability for the package holiday market), meetings intermediaries(for example, meeting planning companies) sometimes cannot recover VAT for the conference packages they sell to corporate clients, nor can they charge VAT to clients.

As a result, clients may effectively pay more to book a conference through an intermediary because the VAT charged by a hotel (for example) would be recoverable if clients booked it directly. Over the past three years, VAT rates in most EU countries have risen to an average of just over 20%, so the need to avoid this additional cost is greater than ever.

The description above is a gross simplification. Factors governing how much VAT, if any, is recoverable include the nature of the meeting, the components of the meetings package, and where it is being held. Above all, are the venue and supplier contracts signed by the principal (i.e., the client) or the agent? And is the agent disclosed or undisclosed, meaning is the contract visible to all parties?

The good news is that if the contract is set up right, usually by making the principal the signatory, VAT can be charged and recovered by the intermediary, but getting the legalities right is no simple matter. Finding a VAT expert to check your contracts is essential.

Centralizing Supplier Contracts

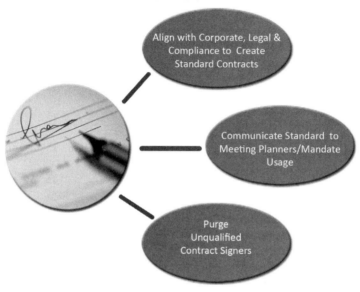

Align with Corporate, Legal & Compliance to Create Standard Contracts

Communicate Standard to Meeting Planners/Mandate Usage

Purge Unqualified Contract Signers

Contractual Risk

Rather better understood among meetings professionals, but not among nonexperts, is the risk of expensive penalties if no one has checked the cancellation and attrition clauses in venue contracts. Once again, this really makes the case for having an SMMP. The SMMP leader can work with the Legal and Compliance departments within the corporation to align existing contractual standards and create templates for meeting contracts that minimize or eliminate penalties. Equally important is teaching your organization's meeting planners about those contracts, loading them into your meetings technology platform, and ensuring only the proper individuals have authority to sign them in dealing with hotels. Administrative assistants with no training in contract management should not be signing deals with hotels.

Appropriateness

This is another huge area of legal and reputational risk, especially in America, with the impending introduction of the Physician Payments Sunshine Provisions of US national healthcare reform. This provision of law dictates, among other things, that life sciences and pharmaceutical companies keep strict record-keeping on payments made to healthcare providers invited to meetings and events. The information will be made public. The EU has had similar regulations in place since 2007, leading to strict rules on how much can be spent on conferences in this sector, and even how much can be spent on leisure activities at such meetings.

To make matters more complicated, however, the precise rules vary in each EU member state, and in some, the codes of practice are voluntary, whereas in others (like Italy) they are compulsory. However, even if a company cannot be fined for breaching the codes, its reputation can still suffer. The UK, for example, publicly names and shames companies in breach. Yet again, structured meetings management is essential to ensure compliance.

Away from the pharmaceuticals industry, fears of hostile perceptions, both in the media and among shareholders, of extravagance remain a key concern for meetings organizers. This is one reason why average meetings spend has fallen by double-digit percentages in the last few years.[6]

However, those fears can sometimes produce the opposite effect. A few months ago, a hotel marketing company representative commented on how it offered a British meetings client the choice between a hotel in the UK and one in the Canary Islands. The client chose the former in spite of the latter being cheaper, even after flight costs were factored in. "Tenerife looked too flash," the representative said. "So they booked the UK hotel instead. They didn't want to have to justify the trip."

6 US corporations spent $54.3 billion on meetings in 2009, down nearly 30% from 2008; source: PhoCusWright's Groups and Meetings, "Driving Success in Business Travel's Most Complex Segment," December 2010. In the UK, The 2009 British Meetings & Events Industry Survey reported a 33% reduction in corporate event volumes during that year; source: conworld.net, September 2009.

Looking to get the most accurate picture possible of meeting spend? The answer for many companies is a dedicated corporate meeting card, separate from a corporate travel and entertainment (T&E) charge card. This chapter discusses why a meeting card is so important to SMMPs: a card aggregates meeting spend information across departments, divisions, and operating regions within an organization; offers greater visibility into pure meetings spend for cost control and policy compliance improvement; increases buying leverage with suppliers; pares financial and accounts payable administrative tasks; and ends the need for suppliers to constantly check on payment to invoices. In this chapter, writer Betsy Bondurant, founder and president of Bondurant Consulting and long-time meetings executive in the pharmaceutical industry, offers guidance in picking a variety of card types and elaborates on why meeting cards are also good for suppliers.

Integrating a Meeting Card into Your SMMP

by Betsy Bondurant

First of all, what exactly is a meeting card?

It is a credit card used exclusively for meetings and events spend, such as to pay for the initial deposit required by a hotel, destination management company (DMC), or audio-visual supplier, or to pay off your hotel master account (an account set up by meeting planners at a hotel to which all items are charged for the meeting).

A meeting card is not a purchasing card, otherwise known as a P-card, nor is it a personal T&E card that business travelers carry. A meeting card is different, and yields its own unique and numerous benefits for your organization:

- You gain the ability to aggregate your meeting spend in one place providing greater visibility to your overall program.[7]

---

7 According to "Meetings and Events: Where Savings Meet Success," a 2010 study by CWT Travel Management Institute and StarCite, one of eight ways to maximize meetings and event management is to use "a single mode of payment such as a corporate meeting card for supplier costs and a corporate credit card for attendees' reimbursable expenses."

- The consolidated information on supplier spend can give you increased buying leverage when negotiating with your suppliers.
- You keep the meeting and event spend clean, meaning it is not bundled with individual travel spend, which makes it hard to analyze.
- There are increased efficiencies and cost reductions; for example, by eliminating purchase order (PO), invoice, and check-processing time for your company.
- Your employees spend less time "chasing," or tracking down, unpaid invoices from suppliers (see box) or filing expense reports meetings-related charges.
- Ensures timely billing, reconciliation, and payment.

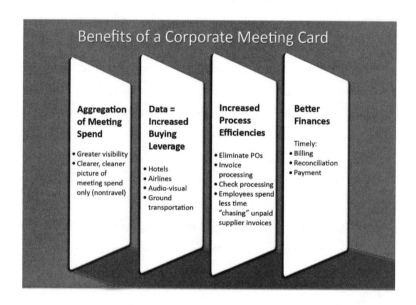

Benefits of a Corporate Meeting Card

Aggregation of Meeting Spend
- Greater visibility
- Clearer, cleaner picture of meeting spend only (nontravel)

Data = Increased Buying Leverage
- Hotels
- Airlines
- Audio-visual
- Ground transportation

Increased Process Efficiencies
- Eliminate POs
- Invoice processing
- Check processing
- Employees spend less time "chasing" unpaid supplier invoices

Better Finances
Timely:
- Billing
- Reconciliation
- Payment

Card Benefits in Action

When evaluating companies that have implemented cards, there's one really interesting case that stands out because the client achieved *substantial* productivity increases and reduced processing time. At that firm, the Finance department helped to determine that the company spent an average $112 to process each supplier PO and issue a check. When using a meeting card, there is no need to initiate a PO or issue individual checks, as you pay all suppliers each month via a single billing statement.

Once the company started using the card, they totaled up how many transactions were on each card per month. Some planners only had 15 transactions, while others had 30 or more (the entire planning team had on average 110 transactions). When the total number of transactions was multiplied by that $112 benchmark cost to process POs and checks, the savings came out to $14,000 cost avoidance per month, or $168,000 annually. This was a significant savings metric to add to the dashboard that went to senior leadership.

"Chasing" unpaid supplier invoices adds hours monthly and days annually to a meeting planner's time.

Typically, planners get calls from hotels, DMCs, or other suppliers seeking information on the payment status of an invoice sent. Or they have to make calls to vendors in the days or weeks following an event to get final bills. Planners must then track down the information with their A/P department or investigate internally within the financial system.

With a meeting card, once you reconcile the invoice, you can tell the supplier it is approved and it is immediately processed and paid. There is no second-guessing when they'll receive payment.

CASE STUDY

Deploying a meeting card program has been critical for one major fast-food chain. With meeting activity being extremely decentralized throughout its regional sales divisions, rolling out a card program has helped the corporation begin to consolidate its spend while building acceptance and adoption for its SMMP. The event organizers and planners enjoy the convenience of the meeting cards and freedom from the hassles of invoice processing.

Additionally, the centralized meeting planning team had been tracking time spent on various aspects of the planning process. One of the process categories was "reconciliation and payment," and it found that with the implementation of the meeting card, the time spent to reconcile and pay dropped by about 20%. That essentially freed up the total of one full-time employee for a year.

Yes, the planners still had to reconcile the supplier invoice, but it was a much simpler process with the card: once the charges were authorized by the planner, the supplier applied the charges to the card. Everyone knew that the supplier had been paid, and in record time! Thus there was no need for time-consuming, follow-up calls from the supplier to the planner looking for payment (and subsequently from the planner to Accounts Payable to check on the status of payment).

Get Leadership, Stakeholders on Board

If you already have some of the elements of a strategic meetings management program (SMMP) in place, the benefits outlined above are typically enough to get the endorsement from senior leadership to move forward with a meeting card. It's likely that you will work with someone in your Finance department, the T&E card administrator and Procurement to help determine if your card should be issued by the same company as the existing T&E or P-card issuer. There may be a compelling argument to keep it with the existing provider.

For example, the card company may be willing to pay a higher rebate, as it also issues a P-card and T&E card to the company. Or there could be just as compelling an argument to go to another issuing company. Perhaps another issuer has more global acceptance levels among merchants. Also, the meeting manager should realize that when it comes to making the decision on which card to use, there will likely have to be much more input from other areas outside of the meeting organization, such as Finance.

Additionally, there very likely could be a role for the meeting card with the technology you use to support your SMMP. Some end-to-end solutions help enhance the reconciliation process and increase data visibility, so it would be wise to keep this in mind as one of your potential business requirements. The bottom line is that you need to select a meeting card that will meet all the business requirements you have identified in order to make your card program successful.

In recent years, there has been a need established to provide a globally accepted card as a key business requirement, as more and more companies are broadening the reach of their programs outside of North America. As more card providers expand their acceptance levels globally, the ability to work with one card has become a reality. That being said, some companies use more than one card to cover different regions of the globe. As long as you are doing a good job of aggregating the data, this solution, although not ideal, can be very workable. The next trend coming to the marketplace is the pin-and-chip design that has been deployed in almost all countries except the US. A few US banks are beta testing the pin-and-chip system this year, so hopefully this will become reality in the not too distant future.

Varied Meeting Card Choices

A meeting card can be appropriate for just about any SMMP. It can be especially helpful for a centralized program where the majority of spend is managed by a few people. In this case, you could easily assign a card to each individual meeting planner in the group, who would then have the responsibility for using the card and handling the reconciliation according to your standard operating procedures (SOPs).

Likely there may be other power users in your organization who would be issued a meeting card, in addition to those in the meeting department. There are other examples of card deployment where a card is issued for each meeting. This sounds as if it could be cumbersome but, in fact, is usually a pretty automated process, depending on the provider. Once the meeting and related budget is approved, the card administrator can go online to the program management section of the issuer and automatically request a card for the meeting planner. The planner usually has a card within twenty-four to forty-eight hours.

The amount of funds available on the card is equal to the meeting budget, which really helps with controlling spending. If more money is required because of a change in scope of the meeting, the card limit can be increased through preexisting approval procedure. If you have an outsourced program where your planners are third-party professionals, you can still implement a card program and have it managed by the third party. Most suppliers embrace the meeting card because it gives them speedy payment for services, even though they are paying a nominal service fee to the card issuer. Many suppliers make the strategic decision to accept the meeting card because it is a requirement of becoming a preferred supplier for a specific organization. But once they integrate meeting card acceptance into their method of operation, they see how it maximizes and improves their client relationships.

Preventing Fraud

SOPs were mentioned earlier. This is one major aspect of implementing a meeting card that cannot be overlooked. Internal auditing departments, in addition to the card provider and corporate program administrator, can develop well-thought-out SOPs that protect their companies from fraudulent use of cards. Some factors to consider when developing meeting card SOPs:

- Clearly identify what suppliers and types of charges are appropriate for the meeting card, and specify those that are not.
- Assign monthly spend limits to planners based on the scope of meetings they typically plan.
- Develop a reconciliation review process to be administered by supervisors.
- Identify cut-off dates for online reconciliation and approval in alignment with the corporate payment timeline.

Preventing Meeting Card Fraud

It is important to remember that card data is a tremendous enhancement to the overall understanding of your SMMP spend. The card data reflects actual spend (versus bookings only) and supplies another layer of business intelligence that helps to maximize your buying power, provides clarity to spending patterns of those utilizing the card, and helps to control expenditures by placing spend limits by planner, meeting, or supplier type.

Data is power. Meeting cards, and the business intelligence they provide, are truly powerful.

Going global with your strategic meetings management program (SMMP) is a 24/7 job, and not just because of the variance in the world's time zones. In this chapter, read about how a growing number of companies are taking up the challenge to expand holistic meetings management beyond their headquarters to operating regions around the globe—picking technology that works cross-border, making room for different cultural and business norms, tailoring communication to a variety of audiences, and providing training to make their programs work. In this chapter, StarCite's Kevin Iwamoto draws on his observations made traveling the world evangelizing about meetings management, as well as his many years of previous experience managing a multinational travel program at a technology firm. Iwamoto presents winning ways in which meetings managers can successfully grow their programs globally.

Taking Your Strategic Meetings Management Program Global

by Kevin Iwamoto

We live in a world where change is the constant we can rely upon. What we often consider static is, in fact, fluid. Strategic meetings management (SMM) is no exception. It knows no boundaries and continues to advance and evolve.

Even though it was conceptualized and developed in the US as a business science for managing the full spectrum of meetings management processes, companies all over the world, including firms with a global presence, are increasingly turning to SMM to help buffer against fluctuating meeting costs, implement centralized budgeting and sourcing, increase meetings and travel compliance, and mitigate corporate risk. SMM gains can be multiplied by expanding the scope of their programs on a global basis; for example, using global meetings spend data to obtain greater supplier leverage or negotiate standardized terms and conditions in meetings contracts.

Recent research shows that half of meeting managers polled in the US have responsibility for meetings in their home country as well as other regions.[8] For the past decade, strategic meetings management

---

8   PhoCusWright's Groups & Meetings, "Driving Success in Business Travel's Most Complex Segment," December 2010.

programs (SMMPs) and the meetings technology that supports them, have helped countless companies reduce costs and set new standards of meetings management efficiencies, for example, by:

- Streamlining sourcing and procurement with mandated request for proposals
- Centralizing budgeting and planning
- Tightening the meetings approval process
- Creating and strengthening meetings policy and using preferred suppliers
- Simplifying registration and attendee management
- Streamlining payment to suppliers and reconciliation
- Facilitating comprehensive data analysis, reporting and applying formal return on investment (ROI) metrics

Today, while just a minority of companies has embraced all the components of an SMMP, most companies have implemented at least some portion of a program, according to a recent study.[9] And, while implementing an SMMP systemwide across a company's domestic operations comes with a variety of challenges (obtaining executive buy-in; measuring total spend, standardizing processes across departments or divisions; gaining acceptance and adoption among users and, of course, implementing and tracking the program), taking an SMMP to different operating regions or globally comes with its own unique set of hurdles. But a growing number of companies are proving these are challenges that can be met and overcome with success.

9 PhoCusWright's study reveals 28% of 226 meeting overseers polled have implemented all seven key components of an SMMP, while 95% have implemented at least one module of an SMMP.

Avoid Cultural Conflicts

One of the biggest hurdles a meeting manager will experience in developing a global SMMP is incorporating cultural differences into a workable program. The end goal should be to incentivize meeting planners across an organization to comply with the company's rules on sourcing and preferred suppliers, using meetings technology, employing your company's standard contracts, and ensuring adherence to global brand standards.

Incentivizing Global Participation in SMMP

But you don't want to build a Berlin Wall that blocks your path of progress with insensitive and/or unrealistic directives that ignore unique characteristics of how regional planners put together events or how managers oversee local programs. You'll just add fuel to resistance. It is important to do your research beforehand to understand the unique aspects of planning and procuring meetings across global regions. Incorporate your international colleagues' current methods of planning and management in whatever way possible into your global SMMP. And even though you have a "centralized" program, a one-size-fits-all approach may not work. Remember, the goal is to increase efficiencies and align meeting program goals and objectives with the company's overarching corporate goals and objectives.

For example, there are some very valuable cultural truisms that can aid SMMP adoption. Take the Asia/Pacific region. Administrative assistants at Asian corporations hold enormous influence, and it would be foolish to underestimate their potential impact based on their titles. Assistants control the schedules of senior executives, meeting, travel, or purchasing directors, as well as any communication sent from them. If you are a meetings manager with a multinational corporation, becoming an ally with these assistants can help you with everything from getting regional support for your SMMP expansion to communicating the goals of the new program to company planners and other stakeholders.

In Australia, you may find yourself at luncheon meetings where wine is served. While imbibing in spirits midday at a meeting may be inappropriate at American corporations in the US, you have to create policies that are flexible for each country or region in a global SMMP. Having a no-alcohol policy during work hours may be acceptable in the US, but in some countries it may be counter to local traditions and customs. This example also shows you the limitations you may have in trying to centralize and standardize all meeting planning and why your program cannot overlook local control and expertise in building programs. Planning can be localized, but your global meetings technology solution can be the central portal to manage policies, approvals, meetings registrations, budgets, and data.

Europe, despite its currency unification, is another region where each country's rules, regulations, and cultural practices (some of them existing for thousands of years) differ greatly. For example, there is a seemingly natural aversion to commoditization and US-centric programs, with their emphasis on compliance to centralized processes. You should understand those differences before going in, and make sure you have the authority and charter to make changes happen. Collaborating with and asking for feedback, input, and advice from local managers goes a long way toward establishing internal stakeholders and cheerleaders to support your charter and mission for a globalized initiative like SMMP.

Select One Technology Solution That Works Universally

A technology solution that supports companies' wide array of needs, whether they do business in Minneapolis or Mumbai, is the key ingredient in building a global SMMP. When you are comparing meetings technology solutions, here are a few "must haves" to include in your request for proposal (RFP) to vendors:

- Operability in multiple languages
- Operability in multiple currencies for sourcing, back-office, and reporting purposes
- The ability to build in unique routing rules to meet regional legislative requirements, multicountry tax laws, etc., especially those that exist in regulated industries such as the pharmaceutical and life-sciences industries
- The ability to establish unique configurations to match regional requirements, the use of regionally based meetings or travel partners, or other unique processes
- The ability to support an expanding group of meetings attendees and planners
- Twenty-four-hour availability of support (real, live people to talk to) for meeting planners or attendees who need help in any region of the globe
- Remote accessibility to the technology and seamless updates via the cloud or software as a service
- Access to references and customer contact information, especially from the technology company's customers who have deployed their SMMPs globally

The Importance of Communicating and Training

SMMP Communication/Training Objectives

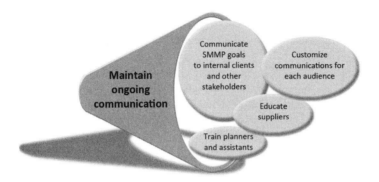

Real success in expanding your SMMP requires continuous train-ing, communication of goals, and a statement of support from your CEO or another senior executive. As part of a European-based financial institution's phased global rollout of its SMMP,[10] the financial services firm trained professional planners to use its chosen meetings technol-ogy. The meetings technology platform served as a central web portal for planners and procurement folks to use via a single point of access.

Again, underscoring the importance of addressing cultural differ-ences, this European bank encountered resistance from suppliers in Germany who were unused to processing meetings proposals electronically. As a result, the bank used workshops, town hall meetings,

---

10 "Bank Migrates Meeting Methods," *Business Travel News*, March 16, 2009.

and training sessions to introduce the new e-RFP technology to its supplier partners, advising how to properly respond. What's important to note is that the bank replicated this best practice in all geographic regions to ensure global program success, taking into account the various cultural business differences from region to region.

This company's story dramatizes the importance of educating and working with business partners as well as internal stakeholders. Aside from meeting planners and senior executives, consider communicating your new global SMMP goals and directives to clients, procurement allies, the Travel department, administrative assistants, Human Resources (HR), occasional planners, Legal, and Finance.[11] Tailor your communication to fit different audiences. For example, if part of your audience is Procurement and Finance executives, address cost savings, cost avoidance, and risk mitigation that can be achieved by going global. On the other hand, if you are reaching out to HR, speak about employee safety and risk mitigation benefits. And if you are speaking to executives, focus on top-line objectives, with no more than five high-level bullet points. A senior executive only wants to know the following three things:

1. What's the current situation today?
2. What are you proposing that is going to positively improve the existing situation and the expected timeline for change?
3. How much will your solution or process cost, and what will be the ROI?

---

11 "Who are the Key Stakeholders in Your SMM?," *Strategic Meetings Management*, October 28, 2010.

Communication should be heavy in the initial stages of expanding your program. And you should maintain an ongoing schedule of outreach for each year thereafter, taking into account that, down the line, your company will hire new employees or acquire merger-impacted employees who will need to be educated about your global travel and meetings policies and programs. To stay current, always designate time to update your policies and procedures, too. And another best practice: if your policy is linked with other departments like Finance, HR, Legal, and others, make sure that whenever you update your policy, their policies are current as well, including intranet links to policies information.

Little Things Mean a Lot

Going global involves paying attention to the details just as much as focusing on the grand strategies. Just think of the huge time differences around the world, and that should prepare you for late-night phone conferences, marathon long flights to meet colleagues, as well as utilization of virtual technology for internal team meetings. It can be a twenty-four-hour job. Make plans to employ translators when necessary, and when communicating, be sensitive about using region centric language, acronyms, and expressions. Most people around the world may know what "okay" means, but chances are they will look at you funny if you say or write that an issue is being "put on the back burner."

With a solid plan in place that aims to build enthusiasm and support among colleagues, respects cultural sensitivities as much as possible, provides ongoing education, is bolstered by senior management, and tackles thorny change management issues, your global SMMP will take root and flourish on turf at home and around the world.

The discipline of SMM had its roots in the concept of meetings consolidation. *The mission of every strategic meetings technology program is to gather data and leverage it for visibility, savings, and control. StarCite founder and former CEO John Pino, who is also founder and CEO of i-Meet, a global professional and social network for people who plan and manage meetings and events, discusses foundational technology needs for an effective program and considerations for the future.*

Bringing It All Together: The Importance of Technology

by John Pino

Many progressive professionals in the meetings and events industry today have embraced the concepts around strategic meetings management (SMM). And while there are a number of ways to describe the concept, many of the core aspects are rooted in a vision termed *meetings consolidation*[12] that still rings true today.

Meetings consolidation refers to the systematic collection of data that enables an adoption process for purchasing, servicing, and reporting on a corporation's meeting and event activities. It is embarked on for the express purpose of achieving cost efficiencies/savings, improving service levels and processes, and delivering more transparent visibility into the meeting activities across an enterprise.

There have been many advances to the original concept, and SMM today has evolved into a professional discipline that greatly benefits organizations, particularly those that use meetings and events as part of their operational strategies.

---

12 Meetings Consolidation was originally branded by McGettigan Partners in 1994. This business focus was part of the original launch of StarCite in January 1999. Meetings Consolidation principles (now evolved to be SMM) drove meetings technology development, which continues to this day.

SMM Requires a Holistic Approach

When you start with a clear vision on what should occur, then the required enablers begin to emerge. Nothing is more vital to success than a solid technology foundation. And, just as SMM is a holistic approach to managing meetings, a holistic technology approach to support SMM is also required. It seems curious that anyone would believe that implementing SMM technology on a piecemeal basis would be effective to consolidate data. Therefore, I have always advocated a technology road map based on the holistic approach to SMM. So rather than starting with existing processes and automating them, a better process was envisioned first. Fortunately, with the help of numerous corporations that desired the same strategy and results, a foundation began with the concept of *full process technology*, addressing the key activities that drove the biggest potential results: cost savings, cost avoidance, and ways to support supplier management objectives that are core to any SMM strategy. Meetings are a major indirect spend category for corporations. The deliverables desired center around improving buying, tracking savings, and leveraging spend with suppliers.

An SMM platform technology must go beyond features that benefit a specific meeting, and it must provide a clear and accurate picture of the company's global meetings that business managers expect. This is the difference between a strategic solution (one that helps enterprises achieve their goals *and* processes that drive better meetings and events) versus point solutions (which address tactical pain points, such as attendee management).[13] The right technology must have

13 There is confusion around real cost savings versus operational efficiencies. Point solutions do reduce the cost of administering a meeting, such as reducing the cost of attendee management and servicing. But these costs, when compared to the total meetings budget, generally are low, and the largest meeting components such as hotel accommodations, food & beverage, air tickets, and meeting content make up almost 90% of the spend.

advantages that address the needs of corporate leadership (finance and strategy), but also feature tools to streamline and improve the actual meetings planning process, thereby benefiting planners and attendees.

SMM Technology Basics

The best technologies in the world are useless unless an organization and its users support the business purpose that is enabled and can engage with the new systems and processes as part of their daily routine. People will resist moving to new processes and technologies unless they see the advantages on a personal and business level. Most organizations go through a process that directly or indirectly forces them to address a number of critical components as they seek to manage adoption along the path to SMM.

The first challenge is to communicate the benefits and build excitement internally. To manage meetings as an indirect spending category effectively, you must demonstrate that the processes initiated will get results—that they will be centered around solid procurement processes that provide visibility, savings, and control (VSC). But as is common with VSC initiatives, this can be a two-edged sword. True, data from VSC initiatives is valuable and factual. Data drives responsible ongoing investments, identifies cost-savings potential, uncovers inefficiencies, and exposes decisions that are less than optimal. All of this is positive when viewed with a lens that seeks continuous improvement. That said, not everyone will view VSC initiatives with the same enthusiasm, and getting through that obstacle requires skilled communications and the support of people who understand your vision.[14]

In order to provide a solid foundation, certain critical components are required to drive results. A patched-together collection of point solutions and tools that aren't part of a comprehensive process is not the answer. The best technology rallies around a set of capabilities in its SMM platform that address the essential processes for success. There should be modules that greatly improve the buying process, streamline the meeting planning process, support the registration of attendees, allow for budgeting and reporting, and of course aggregate all the data so that it can be an effective tool for continuous improvement and goal achievement. Here's a look at the right components to consider:

Plan	Budget	Buy	Attend	Pay	Measure
Scope Out; Rationalize Need; Gain Approval	Construct Budgets & Track Spend	Send RFPs to Suppliers Worldwide	Create Custom Sites & Manage Attendees	Use Meeting Card to Pay Costs & Reconcile Expenses	See All Activity & Data in Real-Time
■ Calendar ■ Meeting Request ■ Approvals ■ ROI Calculator	■ Individual Meetings ■ Enterprise ■ Categorize ■ See Variance ■ Integrate	■ Connect to Suppliers ■ Track Utilization ■ Share/Reuse Cancelled Space ■ Leverage	■ Build Attendee Meeting Sites ■ Market Events ■ Connect to Online Air Booking ■ Inventory Control ■ Attendee Data/Compliance	■ Simplify Payment Process ■ Reduce Accounting Costs ■ Track & Consolidate all Meeting Spend	■ Dashboard ■ Reports ■ Enterprise Roll-up ■ Benchmark ■ Department Goals

14 Many SMM initiatives face obstruction due to a lack of understanding on the strategy, and many times are viewed as personal attacks on past efforts, practices, and results achieved by those engaged in meetings planning. Only when the fear is replaced by optimism for improvement can the obstacles around acceptance begin to be removed.

Beyond the Basic

Coverage of the technology basics is a critical aspect of any SMMP program. The most successful SMMPs to date all have one common thread: they considered these elements critical at the onset of their program. But where do we go from here? What are some of the drivers to future changes within SMM technology? To understand this, let's consider some of the challenges.

One challenge is that all users are not the same. The needs of the professional planner are different than those of the casual planner, and meetings have different levels of complexity. So this presents a practical challenge: whether the technology helps planners and managers do their job better and more efficiently and is easy to learn and use. Technologies need to be intuitive in their processes, supported with training and adapted to the particular needs of the user. That is not to say that they aren't robust in the depth of capabilities they offer, but rather they provide methods that assist a user in both simple and sophisticated tasks.

Another challenge is the ability of the technology and its provider to assist with change management. From a technology perspective, this is the ability to tailor the technology to your organization. So, while adoption of best practices is advised, managers still need to adapt the program to their organization's needs. For instance, meeting definitions, budget structures, approval flows, and even the presentation layer are aspects that need to be malleable.

From a change management perspective, the vendor should be able to provide experience and expertise to support how an initiative will be rolled out. Practitioners will tell you that change management is the toughest part of implementing an SMMP. So this is obviously vital to the process and having a strong implementation plan around technology is essential. The best technology companies have always understood this, and they work closely with clients to be sure that the rollout includes all the required components to get off to a strong start. These include technical integrations and links, loading preferred suppliers, setting up data for reporting, global and local-area customizations, and a clear communications strategy so that suppliers can understand and support SMM objectives.

A final challenge is connecting and integrating the SMM technology to the practices, systems, processes, and users within the organization. This helps to establish your program as a natural extension of other institutionalized processes. Users, who are more and more virtual and on the go, need accessible applications in the cloud that can be mobilized.

The Future: Envisioning Better Meetings That Support Business Results

Much has been written and pioneered by industry leaders around the strategic nature of meetings management and the requirement to find alignment with corporate goals and initiatives. In many respects, the industry will continue to lead global organizations in their efforts to create and manage procurement initiatives, data aggregation, and ROI.

The future will include new innovations for SMM. On the technology side, it seems inevitable that social media will play an important role as the workforce continues to embrace its capabilities and effectiveness. So look for much more with global communities, especially those specifically focused on our industry, such as i-Meet.[15] Communities like i-Meet and others will bring relationship management to a new level and further enable global collaboration and a kind of support not seen to date.

15 i-Meet is the world's largest online community for people who plan meetings and events.

Knowledge is power. Regardless of how you chose to use the information, understanding your total spend across both business and meetings travel will pay dividends. Carol Salcito, president of travel management consulting firm Management Alternatives, Inc., provides a guide on how organizations can increase their meetings management prowess by leveraging this information in combination with transient business travel. She discusses the value of the data, strategies to leverage the information, and, equally important, where to find it.

Power Management: Combining Meetings and Business Travel Management

by Carol Salcito

When you were in school, did you ever have the experience of being unprepared for a test? Maybe you knew only half the answers because you studied only part of the material. That's a lot like sitting down with a preferred hotel supplier to negotiate for a season of room rate discounts—but using only half your company's lodging expenditures for leverage. The reality is that's what most companies are doing today. Maybe that is because all you know about is pure business travel and not meetings travel spend, or how much your company is spending on hotels when staff, customers, or others are booking room nights as part of a meeting.

Why is meetings spend so often neglected, especially when it is such a huge part of overall business travel? One study,[16] funded by the U.S. Travel Association and the Destination & Travel Foundation, found that three hundred US executives surveyed reported 77% of

---

16 "The Return on Investment of U.S. Business Travel," Oxford Economics USA, 2009.

In a recent poll, almost half (46%) of travel, procurement, and/or meeting managers who had started to integrate management of transient and meetings travel, or were considering it, expected to reduce costs by 1%–20%. Meanwhile, one in five expected greater returns, with the majority, 17%, foreseeing savings of 21%–30%.

business travel spend by type of trip was for some type of meeting. The largest category was sales meetings, at 34%.

Implementing centralized processes for managing both business and meetings travel not only gives you and your organization greater leverage to negotiate with travel suppliers, but also empowers you to make smarter budgeting and forecasting decisions. You get a true picture of total spend so you can tackle areas of costs you haven't yet begun to control.

Where to Get the Data?

Compelling evidence shows the opportunities available to corporations that want to maximize their business travel and meetings spend for greater savings and control. In a 2011 survey[17] of nearly two hundred travel management professionals globally, among the top ten priorities for travel buyers were driving air and ground transportation savings; optimizing hotel spend; further consolidating the travel program; and tackling meetings and events. A 2010 survey[18] that also polled two hundred travel, procurement, and/or meeting managers found that 18% had integrated business travel and meetings management, while a combined 50% indicated they had

17 Carlson Wagonlit Travel's third annual survey, "Travel Management Priorities 2011: Insights into the Rebound."
18 *Integration of Corporate Travel & Meetings Management*, November 2010; Research sponsored by ACTE, American Express, IMEX Group, and StarCite

started to integrate or were considering the move but had not yet begun.

But where should you start looking for the data you'll need to combine to improve your negotiations and increase your overall savings?

Capturing transient business travel information has long been a challenge. Even when travel management companies or online tools are designated for use, people still book outside the system. Corporate cards may be issued, but people use personal cards or cash instead. It is inherently difficult to capture supplier data from expense reports. Still, these reports represent excellent sources of business travel information. Promoting compliance and utilization of the tools you've deployed improves the quality of the information.

However, as most people realize, meetings information goes beyond traditional business travel sources and may be found in purchase orders, check requests, and other sources because services are often purchased via alternate methods. If you have implemented a strategic meetings management program, then you are likely using a system like StarCite to get visibility of the meetings occurring and using its capabilities to manage budgets and capture meeting expense information for vendors. You can also then leverage credit card and meeting card sources to pull in actual cost information. The reconciliation process helps to ensure full accounting. Moreover, using attendee management tools aids in getting compliance for use of your online booking tools.

Using electronic tools is vastly superior to using manual systems; electronic tools cut down and eliminate potential data entry errors, making your data even more accurate. It's critical, too, to set up electronic systems to break down expense data into various categories, reflecting spend on such things as room nights, restaurants, meeting space, and audio-visual.

Tying It All Together: What to Do with Your New Data

Now that you've collected both meetings and transient business travel data and can see the overall picture of information, the next step is about finding synergies with suppliers you use.

Clients should dissect spend information to determine how they're doing business with key suppliers. Then meet with sales reps from airlines, hotels, and other vendors to find ways you can capitalize from your relationships. For example, you could discover that you're only doing one meeting per year with an XYZ property, but you're also giving them a thousand room nights in regular business travel spend. That's synergy you can then build upon, and you should be able to leverage some improved buying power.

Once you can see all your information in one place, you may want to consider going out to bid to find new suppliers. Or, if your data reveals you're using multiple suppliers in one particular location, consider paring that number in order to gain more, concentrated buying leverage. A caveat, though: make sure you're not eliminating vendors that are in any way unique in providing services you require (and at the right price), such as a certain type of audio-visual technology.

The Voice of Authority: Senior Management Support

Once you've analyzed your data and created set program goals, the next step involves change management and encouraging employees to utilize the new preferred supplier agreements. Enlist the backing of a senior executive when you're embarking on a new course to consolidate travel and meetings management. It's a wise idea. A signed directive by the senior executive saying that cooperation among all parties is expected is an effective way to override what often has become a very personal experience for travel managers or meeting planners. For example, in many companies, buyers habitually use their own favorite suppliers or travel management companies (TMCs), despite the existence of officially designated hotels and agencies.

If you can get the signature of a CEO, COO, or CFO on something that says "Here's why we're doing this—and we *will* do it," then you're convincing people that this is the right thing to do for your company. If it fits your culture, you can even go as far as having senior management pronounce that after three, two, or even one time ignoring new policies, individual travelers won't be reimbursed or meeting planners will face repercussions.

Communicate Well, and Do It Often

Good communication is a great way to manage change management when it comes to centralizing transient and meetings travel. It's always best to tell your travel or meeting planners *why* something is happening as well as the details about *what* is happening. If the economic climate is challenging, emphasize that it's being done to benefit the company's bottom line. Individuals will understand, too, because they will learn that changes are happening to prevent layoffs. Use every method of communication you would use to announce something, say, as important as a change in your healthcare plan. Blast it in every possible way; for example, through emails, webinars and messages on travel portals.

When centralizing transient and meetings travel, don't forget to enlist the aid of your travel partners; for example, TMCs and your company's preferred hotels. Make sure they understand they're accountable. Say, "Here's the objective of our corporation. If someone other than the following individuals contact you to set up a meeting, I need to know about it. If you don't let me know, you run the risk of losing us as a client overall." Show them samples of standard contracts and spell out who can sign.

Integration Is a Job Never Completed

Running a consolidated business travel and meetings operation is quite a challenge since, for many companies, meetings management is still the last frontier of overall travel management.[19] The rewards are improved savings, efficiencies, greater supplier buying power, and new levels of cost control. But travel, meetings, and procurement managers need to continually communicate program benefits, track their efforts, and share program successes with senior management. Never take it for granted that once you put something into place, it is the end of the project.

19 Only 28% of companies have implemented all seven of strategic meetings management's key modules, as defined by the Global Business Travel Association, according to a survey of 226 meeting overseers in PhoCusWright's *Groups and Meetings*, "Driving Success in Business Travel's Most Complex Segment," December 2010.

Technology has impacted every aspect of our lives, and meetings are no different. Today, many people work from virtual offices, access corporate networks via virtual private networks, and have organized virtual meetings. Debi Scholar, president of the Scholar Consulting Group and former co-chair of the GBTA's Groups and Meetings Committee, provides a comprehensive guide about virtual meetings—how to develop a strategy for managing them and incorporating them within your strategic meetings management program. With virtual meetings increasingly supplanting and/or complementing meetings travel, this is a must—read chapter for meetings professionals who are intent on saving their companies money and making life easier for attendees.

Crafting a Virtual Meeting and Event Strategy

by Debi Scholar

There's no doubt that virtual meetings are on the rise and will continue to be used more by planners. But not all perceive the same definition or expect the same services when hearing the term *virtual meeting* or *virtual event* (VME).

Many meeting planners today are struggling with how virtual meetings and events fit within their strategic meetings management programs (SMMPs). Fortunately, many of the tools we used to gain visibility, savings, and control into meetings easily apply to virtual meetings as well. For instance, using policy to define virtual meeting categories or simply capturing what virtual meetings are occurring via a meeting request are simple ways to begin.

Ultimately though, virtual meetings and associated technologies should be a critical component to a strategic meetings management (SMM) strategy. Doing so can expand your organization's options to communicate and broaden a Meeting or Travel department's toolbox of planning solutions.

Understanding Virtual Meeting Technology

Three tiers of VMEs offer different experiences for attendees and require various levels of support to be successful.

Virtual Meeting/Event Service Tiers

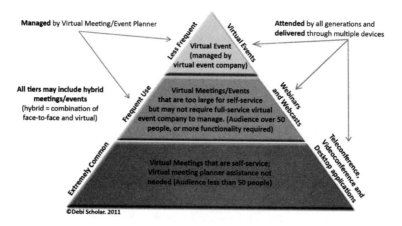

©Debi Scholar. 2011

Tier 1:
Teleconference, Videoconference, and Desktop Applications

The most common virtual meetings are delivered by technologies such as videoconferencing, Skype, GoToMeeting, Webex, LiveMeeting, etc. Often, these technologies are used for meetings with less than fifty attendees and can be easy to set up. These tools have become common in the home and business environment. All the options available within the first tier can be classified as *collaboration solutions* where each attendee may have the opportunity to present to the entire group, also known as *few-to-few* technology.

Tier 2:
Webinars and Webcasting

This category of virtual meetings requires some level of expert assistance and supplier intervention, usually because of a higher number of attendees or the level of functionality desired. Some of the same suppliers that offer the first tier of services may offer more enhanced services. Meetings or events using this kind of technology, also known as *few-to-many* automation, may feature more than fifty people and usually require a couple of days to up to a few weeks to organize properly.

Behind the scenes, the difference between the first and second tier of virtual meetings is the level of technical and planning support needed. While technology support is needed to deliver the content and support the connectivity, a VME planner provides preparation services such as project management, communications and social media, content development and formatting, rehearsals and reporting. This role may be an internal or external resource, because meeting planners who provide services for face-to-face meetings can also learn to deliver virtual meetings.

Tier 3:
Virtual Events

The third and most complex tier of virtual events requires a high level of expert assistance because it may incorporate multiple technologies from the first and second tier that are launched from a virtual technology company's proprietary technology platform. Whether it is a convention/exhibit, trade show, job fair, expo, symposium, or other type of event, the technology supplier will provide an experienced team to lead the development and delivery of the client's virtual event. Some virtual events may be in 3-D and often provide an immersive experience for attendees; yet these events may require months to produce. A VME planner will be needed and may work side by side with a virtual event production coordinator due to the increased volume of both content and production complexity.

Why Use Virtual Meetings and Events?

VMEs can provide numerous benefits to your organization and attendees. Some face-to-face meetings are complemented with virtual meetings, also known as *hybrid meetings*, and some virtual meetings replace face-to-face meetings to reduce the cost of the meeting, broaden the reach to more attendees, or increase the speed to market. A hybrid meeting may reduce a four-day, face-to-face meeting to a two-day, face-to-face event with virtual meeting components to fulfill the four-day content requirements.

To drive adoption toward using virtual meetings, an organization may want to communicate the benefits of using virtual technologies to its staff so they recognize the delivery medium as a win-win for all involved (and a plus for the environment). Benefits to note when discussing the need to move toward virtual meetings/events are listed in the following table.

Benefits of Virtual Meetings & Events		
Provides Better Access to Content	Improves Scalability and Reach	Dramatically Improves Measurement
• Allows immediate immersion into visual, listening and participative environments with people who are not nearby; • Provides immediate access to subject matter experts, multiple presenters from numerous locations and more spontaneous and immediate decisions in lieu of planned meetings; • Provides for replay/archive capabilities for people who are unable to be present or want to replay the on-demand archive; • Provides multiple language options	• Removes the distance for global workforces, clients and markets; • Offers scalability so that large meetings can still "fit" without having to reserve more rooms; • Provides for more people to attend trainings and workshops that could not attend based on travel costs; • Improves work/life balance and the ability to provide attendees with the option of avoiding business travel when possible; • Provides a safe environment for people who may want to discuss topics but are uncomfortable in doing so with an audience in a room or a meeting filled with people they may not know; • Provides an anonymous environment to obtain survey results by using VME polling features	• Provides for tracking of multiple metrics, including attendance during live and archived sessions, poll/survey compliance statistics, and activity data to track what users actually do within the platform; • Improves consistency in branding and marketing; • Cuts the carbon emissions and environmental impact of travel; • Cuts non-productive traveling and flight time and travel expenses; • Reduces telecom costs with a unified communications strategy

@ Debi Scholar 2011

When to Use Virtual Meetings and Events

VMEs will provide the best delivery method for many meetings, but they may not be the right answer for all meetings. Your answers to the following questions will help determine whether to go virtual or face-to-face:

1. What is the general meeting type?
2. What is the general purpose of the meeting?
3. What is the expected outcome and how will it be measured?

Meeting/Event Types

The most common types of virtual meetings are internal meetings, general business meetings, training programs, ongoing customer/client meetings, and supplier meetings. Gaining ground but less common, virtual technologies may be used for important (or new) client meetings, recruiting, interviewing, exhibits, conferences, conventions, and sponsorships. Rarely are retreats, incentives or celebratory events delivered through a virtual medium. However, all of these common face-to-face meeting types can be supplemented with virtual sessions to progressively immerse attendees in the meeting experience.

Virtual Meeting/Event Purpose

A virtual meeting is a good option when the meeting sponsor or planner wants to share information, communicate, demonstrate, motivate, offer subject-matter expertise, sell, present, and educate. In contrast, face-to-face meetings may be better if the meeting sponsor or planner wants to discuss sensitive issues and view the attendees' body language or reactions, build team camaraderie, strive for 100% engagement during presentation of complex topics, deliver to locations with unstable connectivity, or manage cultural norms with some countries that may not be receptive to VMEs.

Measuring Virtual Meeting/Event ROI

A meeting's content and messaging are more important than the delivery medium. VMEs are not about the technology, but rather about bringing together attendees virtually to accomplish a goal. All the creativity that event organizers bring to a face-to-face meeting can be repackaged in a virtual environment. VME planners must learn how to add the human touch to virtual meetings by consciously creating an interactive environment where attendees have opportunities to engage as though they are mingling in a hotel hallway or meeting room. However, it is very challenging to measure interactivity levels in a hotel hallway or meeting room, whereas in a virtual environment it is much easier to gauge these informal actions.

Most VME organizers need to prove an ROI and should identify the expected benefits and measurements before planning the meeting or event. For the most part, meetings and events are held to communicate, motivate, educate, celebrate, evaluate, generate revenue, or regenerate the workforce through recruiting. Consider the following measurements to calculate ROI for a virtual meeting or event:

How to Measure Virtual ROI		
Goal	Define objective	Measurement
Communicate	Was the communication used and understood?	Measure the effects of the communication efforts. For example, if a business meeting was held to discuss a new project, the measurement could be the success of the project completion as evaluated by the project sponsor.
Motivate	Did the attendees change or improve behavior through motivation?	Measure the effects of the improved behavior such as an increase in policy usage.
Educate	Did the attendees learn something that would reduce cost or risk, improve productivity or quality, or generate more sales?	Measure the effects of the education, including an increase in productivity.
Celebrate	Did the attendees feel appreciated?	Measure the effects of the perceived value of the celebratory event. The measurement could be the increase in accomplishments throughout the year or the perceived feeling that the attendees had during the event.
Evaluate	Did the attendees evaluate the service or product as expected and provide the needed feedback?	Measure the depth of the attendee feedback.
Generate Revenue	Did the event help generate more revenue?	Measure the effects of the leads generated, resulting sales or revenue generated.
Regenerate the workforce through recruiting	Did the organization hire more staff?	Measure the effects of the recruiting and interviewing efforts: the number of subsequent interviews held or the number hired who attended the job fair.

© Debi Scholar 2011

Capturing VME Metrics

Depending on the type of VME you plan, functionality requirements can be simple or complex, similar to face-to-face meeting needs. As a result, it is common to use multiple suppliers. However, that can lead to disparate data collection, especially for large organizations. A VME best practice is to use a central data repository for all VME requests, approvals, attendee management, budgeting, and reporting so that the meetings organization can report the VME metrics side by side with the face-to-face meeting/event metrics.

Capturing and Reporting Virtual Meeting and Event

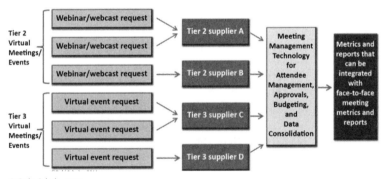

© Debi Scholar 2011

Create a VME Strategy

Creating a VME strategy provides guidance for your organization leaders, meeting requesters, internal and external suppliers, and attendees. This strategy addresses how to reserve, who can support and supply, and how funding is managed for virtual meetings. The best strategy includes direction for all three tiers of VMEs; it also establishes that strategy development is through a team of stakeholders from IT, procurement, training and development, marketing, travel, and meetings management.

Technology support may be owned by IT, yet the meetings, marketing, and training and development teams should be included to build the virtual meeting environment and culture. Implementing a virtual meeting culture requires a balance from all business units to ensure the success of these initiatives. Usually, the objective is to lower operating costs by minimizing the administration and support by centralizing the function with the meetings department. The virtual meeting management process requires well-managed standard operating procedures, trained services roles, communication, and the realization of benefits through comprehensive metrics. Technology is only the enabler, not the solution. As such, the management of VME services should not reside in IT.

By centralizing the management of VMEs, you:

- Support the customer by acting as the single point of contact for all meetings
- Eliminate some face-to-face meetings with a recommended hybrid or virtual approach

- Reduce the costs of meetings by eliminating or decreasing travel, facility costs, and expenses
- Build leverage with preferred virtual meeting suppliers
- Ensure consistency and quality in VME delivery
- Drive adoption through use of subject matter expertise and support services
- Allow for tracking and measuring virtual meeting volume and spend

Roles and Responsibilities

A virtual meeting and event governance structure facilitates timely decision making by the right team, at the right staff level, for seamless services delivered to meeting requesters. As such, there are various roles that may be needed for an organization to provide comprehensive VME services. Here are some examples:

- Information Technology: may manage the relationship with technology suppliers from a contract, support, and service-level agreement perspective.
- Procurement: may manage the request for proposal and contracting process along with stakeholders from IT, Marketing, Training and Development, Meetings and Events, and Travel.
- Training and Development: may manage tools for e-learning or may have a key stakeholder role in the virtual meetings and events initiative.

- Marketing: a key stakeholder in the VME initiative; may be utilizing online events or technologies as part of its lead generation activities.
- Finance: a key stakeholder to support VME payments and reconciliations (or this task may be assigned to the meeting requestor or the meetings team).
- Content Contributor/Content Collector: may own or be responsible for creating and/or collecting the content and messages that will be delivered. This role may be part of the meeting sponsor's team or may be part of the Meetings and Events team.
- Meetings and Events and/or Travel: may manage the service delivery of VMEs. When meeting and event requests are generated and surge into the meetings team (internal staff or outsourced), the meeting planner should offer or recommend VMEs as viable solutions when applicable.

Interacting with
Virtual Meeting/Event Suppliers

VME suppliers offer wide-ranging functionality and capabilities, just like suppliers in the face-to-face meetings environment. It is best to identify the common virtual meeting/event needs with the key stakeholders and use a request for proposal process to find preferred suppliers. Yet, if the organization already has preferred VME suppliers selected, or if the organization is moving toward unified communications, then reach out to those suppliers first to learn about their services.

Many organizations already have TelePresence (virtual meetings featuring life-size images of participants, high-definition video, and high-fidelity audio) studios or other production studios that should be considered before using external suppliers.

If an organization plans to outsource its VME planning and needs to further identify the VME capabilities of its meeting management suppliers, add the following sections to the meeting management request for proposal (RFP):

- Describe your virtual meeting planning capabilities, and list the resources most frequently used, in-house and subcontracted, for webcasts, videoconference, and other virtual meeting technologies. Provide detail on your abilities to recommend and support our virtual meeting and event needs.

- Describe the method you use to recommend a virtual meeting over a face-to-face meeting and the process used to access meetings technology.

- How many clients do you provide virtual meetings for?

© Debi Scholar 2011

Driving Virtual Meeting/Event Adoption

If you build the strategy and obtain the technology, will your audience use it? No, not unless you provide high-quality meetings and events that are engaging and interactive. To help change attitudes and behaviors about VMEs in your organization, consider these strategies:

- *Obtain leadership support.* Leadership plays a critical role in communicating the importance of the VME strategy. In addition, leadership endorsement sets an example for how people will be expected to behave in the future.
- *Practice effective communications.* Effectively informing people of what to expect (and how it fits logically into business unit strategies) will increase the likelihood that the VME strategy will be accepted.
- *Articulate roles and responsibilities.* The VME implementation will change how people work, network, and meet. A clear articulation of future roles and responsibilities will contribute to the successful acceptance of VME processes.
- *Identify competencies.* As roles and responsibilities change, the capabilities and skills necessary to perform them will also change. For example, people will need to know how to collaborate with peers live online and focus on the virtual environment without multitasking and losing site of the meeting or learning objectives. Identifying competencies and developing education surrounding the initiative is imperative for leadership as well as participants.

- *Measure performance.* Measuring performance plays a critical role in shaping how people behave. The data will also provide corrective feedback and motivate the adoption of your VME strategy.
- *Reward high performers.* Rewards and recognition amplify the effectiveness of leadership, communications, and performance measures recommendations. Rewards and recognition also serve to entice and reinforce the adoption of new behaviors.

Creating a Virtual Meeting/Event Policy

A VME policy should be created, or it may be a subsection of the overall meeting policy. The VME policy should instruct meeting sponsors/planners to consider whether business objectives can be accomplished more economically through the use of a virtual medium. Other elements include registration of all Tiers 2 and 3 VMEs or those requiring technology suppliers within the company's meetings management technology platform and meetings calendar. The policy should also establish which level VMEs should route through the meeting approval process, explain the use of preferred suppliers, provide timelines for registration, and planning support. Detailed language for a VME policy can be found in the web resources links at the end of this chapter.

What's Next in Virtual Meetings?

An emerging trend in VMEs is the introduction and use of unified communications, an all-inclusive service already prevalent at many large organizations. Unified communications includes voice and cellular services, instant messaging, calendaring, email, video telephony, contacts, and virtual meetings and collaboration tools.

When you integrate virtual meetings collaboration tools into a unified communications application, the tools become standard and less likely to be used ad hoc throughout the organization. Unified communications will increase adoption and help make virtual technologies easier to use.

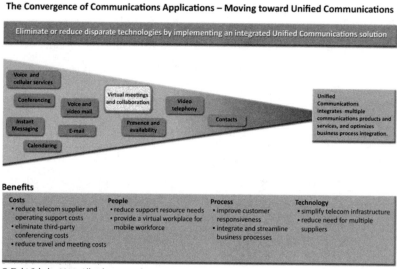

The Convergence of Communications Applications – Moving toward Unified Communications

Eliminate or reduce disparate technologies by implementing an integrated Unified Communications solution

Voice and cellular services
Conferencing
Virtual meetings and collaboration
Voice and video mail
Video telephony
Instant Messaging
Presence and availability
Contacts
Calendaring
E-mail

Unified Communications integrates multiple communications products and services, and optimizes business process integration.

Benefits

Costs	People	Process	Technology
• reduce telecom supplier and operating support costs • eliminate third-party conferencing costs • reduce travel and meeting costs	• reduce support resource needs • provide a virtual workplace for mobile workforce	• improve customer responsiveness • integrate and streamline business processes	• simplify telecom infrastructure • reduce need for multiple suppliers

Resources on Virtual Meetings and Events

http://www.teplus.net

http://www.virtualedge.org/

http://www.webconferencing-test.com/blog/

http://www.linkedin.com/groups/strategic-virtual-meetings-management

Strategic meetings management programs are a key aspect of an organization's broader supplier management strategy within the meeting spend category. Effectively negotiating with suppliers inherently requires that you understand their cost and pricing structures. Commissions and preferential treatment that airlines, hotels, and others provide to travel agencies has long been a source of mystery within the travel, meetings, and events world. Andrew Menkes, CEO and chairman of travel management consulting group Partnership Travel Consulting, provides insight into how to create and leverage a corporate travel department (CTD) into your supplier strategy. As the person who established the first such CTD more than a dozen years ago, Menkes has significant experience in how this can be used to expose and unbundle supplier pricing.

Creating and Leveraging a Corporate Travel Department

by Andrew Menkes

Since the birth of the airline industry and growth of business travel, there have always been travel departments, within organizations, that managed and coordinated employee travel hand-in-hand with outside travel agencies. But Airlines Reporting Corporation® (ARC) and ARC-approved corporate travel departments opened the path for corporations to operate as their own in-house travel agencies: to directly purchase carrier transportation and services for their own employees, owners, and officers, and to receive commissions.

The Birth of CTDs

When I was hired as the first travel manager of New York–based Republic National Bank, I had to plan a large event in Washington, DC, that was hosted every five years by our chairman. After some time sourcing for the right property, I finally narrowed down my choices and met with the hotel's director of sales to review pricing for the presidential suite, plus an entire floor of rooms. When I asked her if the pricing was net, she said, "Yes it is." I asked her what the commissionable rate was for the suites and rooms and she said, "The rates are the same."

I was shocked because I knew that a travel agency could get those same rooms for net. Why not me? I was certainly bringing the same spend to the table. After the initial shock wore off I asked her to explain the rationale and she said that when a corporation contacts the hotel directly the rates are quoted as net; when a travel agency calls the hotel on behalf of the client, they quote the same rates, but pay a 10% commission to the travel agency.

So there it was: I was paying 10% more than an agency would.

As fate would have it, the following week I was taking my Certified Traveler Counselor course in Atlanta, and two of my classmates were the president of ARC and the president of the International Air Transport Association (IATA). We were having a drink at the bar, and I told them I would like my company to be appointed by ARC/IATAN like a travel agency but not open to the public. They each told me in unison that there was no such thing; I ordered another round of drinks and rephrased it. I said, "I would like to be the first corporation to be appointed like a travel agency, but not open to the public. We only want to issue tickets and book rooms for ourselves for business travel."

There was some expected hesitation and concern, especially as to how travel agencies would react to the competition from their own customers. I was well aware that although ARC was owned by a few airlines, their customers were upward of forty thousand travel agencies in the US. IATAN was the international equivalent, so I knew we were treading in unchartered waters.

We had a number of conversations over the next few months, and the solution was to test a pilot of the CTD program, and I guess that made me the test pilot. And so on May 8, 1998, four months later, Republic National Bank was approved as the first CTD in the United States.

How CTDs Changed the Business Travel Landscape

Prior to the CTD program, the financial model between travel agencies and corporations was in the form of a rebate, whereby the agency returned a portion (an agreed-upon percentage) of commissions of airline, hotel, and car rental bookings back to the corporation, usually on a quarterly or semiannual basis. Over the past decade, commissions have been consistently reduced by the airlines, to the point that travel agencies are now charging corporations "management fees," which are deducted from any commissions paid by agencies to their clients. The end result is usually a quarterly invoice, or a minimal return of total commissions earned. There is no reliable audit trail for the commission income in the agency environment.

The CTD program allows corporations to receive all commissions directly from airlines, hotels, and car rental firms (hotels offer the most lucrative revenue stream) and outsource any and all services to one or more travel agencies or travel suppliers. The difference between a CTD and a travel agency is that a CTD is a *purchaser* of travel; a travel agency is a *seller* of travel.

CTD Benefits

The actual benefits derived from a CTD are based in part on the current travel agency arrangement, as well as the overall travel expenditures of the corporation. The CTD does not need to be on the premises of the corporation and the staffing can be agency employees.

The benefits include the following:

- Unbundling of travel agency services, allowing one or more agencies to compete on service and price
- Enhanced cash flow as a result of direct deposit of airline commissions and collection of all paid hotel commissions
- A unique ID number to enhance supplier negotiations, which is retained by the corporation without interruption, regardless of how many suppliers are used

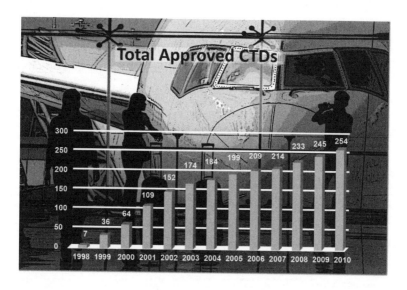

- Improved supplier discounts by eliminating any compensation to the travel agency (by the suppliers)
- Complete data ownership, including access to ARC data provided exclusively to agencies

SMMP Benefits

Over 250 companies have recognized the benefits of the CTD program for their managed travel program; meanwhile, very few companies have implemented a true strategic meetings management program. A CTD program can serve as the bedrock of an SMMP initiative. First, it can greatly aid in discovery of global SMMP data because you can track all supplier spend due to your unique ARC number (assuming your travel is booked through your CTD). As a

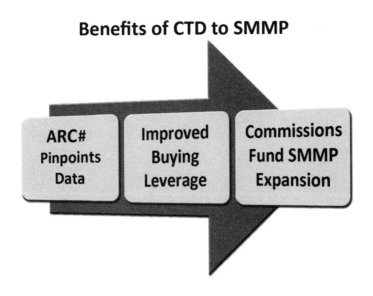

Benefits of CTD to SMMP

ARC# Pinpoints Data

Improved Buying Leverage

Commissions Fund SMMP Expansion

result of this increased knowledge, you gain more leverage for negotiating with hotels and other meeting services providers. Second, your CTD will channel all funds (commissions) directly to your company. And you can budget those funds for paying for SMMP development and expansion. Auditing becomes easier, too, because funds come from a central location.

You are still able to enjoy the flexibility of the CTD program in terms of outsourcing non-core competencies. As an example, if you utilize the services of your travel management company (TMC) to support the logistics of your internal meetings (booking hotel, airfare, and ground transportation), you can continue to do so as a CTD but use your ARC number for receipt of commissions on the sleeping rooms. You will still pay your TMC a fee for services provided, but your company will also have an income stream, for example, hotel commissions, to help offset some of the fees. Owning your own CTD does not mean you have to become or replace a travel agency; it means you are eligible to receive commissions directly.

An SMMP, which includes technology to serve as a central portal, will also enhance compliance to corporate travel programs all around. The meetings technology serves as the central portal to route meetings requests and ensures that appropriate approvals for meetings take place before the travel purchases even begin. Additionally, online registration for meetings can incorporate travel requests providing instant room block information and travel routing.

All too often, meetings are treated like a separate entity across organizations. Administrative employees or marketing associates are tasked with planning a meeting or event. They contact suppliers directly and negotiate contracts for tens of thousands of dollars without the benefit of inside travel knowledge or contract negotiation skills to address cancellation or attrition clauses. CTDs are an ingenious way to stream new sources of funding to your SMMP, increase data visibility and cost control, and power up your bargaining power with suppliers.

AUTHOR PROFILES

Kevin Iwamoto, *Global Leadership Professional (GLP),*
Vice President of Enterprise Strategy, StarCite, Inc.

Kevin Iwamoto is a widely recognized business travel industry leader with more than twenty years of experience managing global corporate travel and meetings programs. He was president and CEO of the Global Business Travel Association (GBTA) and the GBTA Foundation from 2001 to 2003, where he created and launched the GBTA Groups and Meetings Committee and cofounded the global Paragon Partnership organization, forging a relationship between the GBTA and MPI.

Prior to joining StarCite in 2008, Iwamoto spent over ten years at Hewlett-Packard, where, as senior global travel commodity manager, he oversaw development, policy creation, strategy, and supplier management for various global travel spend categories over his tenure, including airlines, car rental, corporate and meetings card, meetings, hotels, and ground transportation. His last portfolio of global corporate spend responsibility was over $1.2 billion.

Among many industry honors and accolades, in 2010 Iwamoto received the Association of Corporate Travel Executive's (ACTE) Distinguished Fellow award, and he was named one of four VIP Movers & Shakers of Strategic Meetings Management by *Corporate*

& Incentive Travel magazine. Iwamoto was awarded the GBTA Industry Icon Award in 2009, an award rarely given and based on lifetime career and industry achievements.

He has been recognized numerous times over the years by *Business Travel News* (*BTN*), including Travel Manager of the Year in 2002, and holds the record for the most Best Practitioner designations— for First On-Line Car Rental Auction in 2000, Innovative Airline Alliance Contracting in 2005, and Meetings Management in 2008. Iwamoto has been named among the Top 25 Most Influential Executives for *BTN* in 2003 and Top 25 Most Influential People in the Meetings Industry by *Meeting News* in 2005. Iwamoto writes Strategic Meetings Management, a popular meetings industry blog.

Betsy Bondurant, *CMP, CMM, Founder, President, Bondurant Consulting*

Betsy Bondurant has over thirty years of experience in corporate meetings and travel management. Bondurant's areas of expertise include strategic planning for global operations, data management, relationship management, SMM technology acquisition, process reengineering, and policy development and implementation. Before establishing her Coronado, CA–based consultancy firm, Bondurant was Procurement director at IHG from 2008 to 2010. Prior to that, Bondurant, for more than fifteen years, was director of Meetings and Trade Shows at Amgen, where she developed and implemented a corporate–wide SMMP.

Among her industry affiliations, Bondurant is a member of the Global Business Travel Association (GBTA). She is currently serving as chair for the Knowledge Advisory Group of Meeting Professionals International. Bondurant was recognized as one of *Business Travel*

News's Best Practitioners of 2002, and in 2004 she was honored as one of *Meeting News*'s 25 Most Influential People in the Meetings Industry.

Louann Cashill, *CMP, CMM, Global Account Manager, Strategic Projects, StarCite, Inc.*

In her current role, Louann Cashill is focused on strategic projects for StarCite. A former corporate meetings program manager, Louann provides proven expertise in deploying the StarCite platform and services to develop, expand, and manage strategic meeting management programs. Cashill has served on several industry boards, is a frequent speaker and contributor to industry events and articles, was named an Industry Changemaker by *Corporate Meetings & Incentives* magazine, and appeared on the cover of its March 2009 edition.

Prior to StarCite, Cashill led Toyota's meeting services and strategic hotel sourcing teams; managed meetings and tradeshows for Amgen; held senior-level positions in luxury hotels, including The Ritz-Carlton and Le Méridien; and worked with Tony Robbins as director of Production, delivering seminars to thousands across the globe.

Carol Salcito, *President, Management Alternatives, Inc.*

For more than thirty years, Carol Salcito has been an instrumental force and source of knowledge in the business travel industry. Since 1992, Salcito has been president of Management Alternatives, Inc., a travel management consultancy based in Norwalk, CT. Salcito leads a multinational team in helping firms manage strategic sourcing and procurement, operations, travel policy creation and implementation, technology, and the overall management of their travel programs, including meetings management.

Before joining Management Alternatives, for sixteen years Salcito worked for United Technologies Corporation. In the last five years of her career there, she was director of Global Travel, with responsibly for the company's multinational travel management program. A long-time member of both GBTA and ACTE, Salcito served for four years on ACTE's board of governors. She has been the chairperson of GBTA's Education Committee in the US, Shanghai, and Brazil, and is a past president of the Connecticut/Westchester chapter.

Salcito is the 1998 recipient of the Professional Service Award from the GBTA Chapter President's Council. *Business Travel News* selected Salcito Travel Manager of the Year while she was at UTC, and she has been named one of the Top 25 Most Influential Executives in the business travel industry. In addition, in 2001 *Travel Agent* Magazine named her one of the Most Influential Female Executives in the Travel Industry.

Linda J. McNairy, *Vice President, Business Development, StarCite, Inc.*

A twenty-plus year veteran of the meetings industry, Linda J. McNairy is driven to constantly make SMM an integral part of organizations' overall success. As vice president, Strategic Partner Management, McNairy leads and manages StarCite's global business strategies with top meeting and travel management suppliers. McNairy joined StarCite in 2005 and advanced from sales to vice president, Global Account Management, heading up a team of twenty who were dedicated to ensuring successful technology deployments and widespread planner adoption levels for StarCite's largest customers.

Her history of industry employment includes management

positions with Navigant Meeting Services (subsequently purchased by Carlson Wagonlit Travel). McNairy's impressive professional accomplishments include serving as the first-ever Allied Member vice chair of GBTA's Groups and Meetings Committee. In her role there, she has been particularly instrumental in developing the strategic meetings management certification, the meetings industry's first professional designation for meeting managers.

She was also a key figure in designing the Strategic Meetings Management Maturity Model, which, developed by the GBTA Foundation in partnership with StarCite, helps organizations assess their current level of meetings management and set goals for advancement. She is also past president of the Indiana chapter of Meeting Professionals International where she served over four years in various leadership positions.

Mike Malinchok, *CPC, President, S2K Consulting, LLC*

Mike Malinchok is president of S2K Consulting, LLC, which focuses on providing consulting services to organizations in the areas of leadership development, executive coaching, change management, and strategic meetings management programs (SMMP). An active member of the Global Business Travel Association (GBTA), Malinchok has worked extensively with the Groups and Meetings Committee in the development of a series of white papers outlining the tenets, benefits, and strategies of what has become known as SMMPs. Mike is a faculty member of the strategic meetings management certification program offered through GBTA.

Malinchok has spent over twenty-five years in the meetings and travel industry in key positions at companies like StarCite, GetThere, BCD Meetings & Incentives, and McGettigan Partners. He has focused most of his career in the area of meetings technology and the business processes surrounding the usage of those technologies. Malinchok is a frequent speaker at many travel industry meetings and events, and is considered one of the foremost experts in the area of SMMPs for corporations.

Malinchok is a graduate of American University in Washington, DC, and he is a Certified Professional Executive Coach, through the Institute for Professional Excellence in Coaching (iPEC). His diverse coaching practice includes one-on-one coaching for professionals and executives seeking peak performance levels in their professional as well as personal lives. His "On Purpose" seminars have been widely recognized for their practical and direct approaches on such topics as Public Speaking Training, Business Discipline Boot Camp, and Transition-to-Transformation 101. His coaching style has been consistently described as insightful, rejuvenating, and thought provoking.

Amon Cohen, *Specialist Business Travel Writer*

Amon Cohen is a specialist business travel writer whose work focuses extensively on corporate travel, meetings management, and supply management issues for publications on both sides of the Atlantic. He is a regular contributor to major industry travel trade magazines such as US-based *Business Travel News* and the UK's *Supply Management* as well as *Buying Business Travel*. In addition, he has written numerous reports and white papers on these topics.

Cohen, who lives in Somerset, UK, also works frequently as a conference moderator for the corporate travel industry and its organizations, including the Association of Corporate Travel Executives, Britain's Guild of Travel Management Companies, the Institute of Travel & Meetings (also UK based) and GBTA Europe. He is a founding partner of specialist media training business Travel Media Training.

George Odom, *President, Strategic Travel & Meetings Group*

As president of Fishers, IN–based Strategic Travel & Meetings Group, George Odom helps corporations manage business travel and meetings expenditures. Odom is best known for his pioneering work incorporating procurement management strategies to corporate travel and meetings. Before founding his own consulting firm, Odom held senior director positions at Advito, the consulting group of BCD Travel and BCD Meetings & Incentives.

Prior to those positions, he led travel and meetings for most of a twenty-nine-year career at Eli Lilly and Company. There, Odom created and implemented key performance indicators (KPIs). Among Odom's industry honors, he was awarded ACTE's Distinguished Fellow Award in both 2003 and 2009. In addition, he served on the association's board of governors. He has been a member of the GBTA's Groups & Meetings Committee and, while there, served on the committee to develop the SMM certification. Odom has also served on the editorial board for *Business Travel News*.

Debi Scholar, *GLP, CMM, CMP, CTE, CTT, and President, Scholar Consulting Group*

Scholar offers guidance to Fortune 1000 and midsize companies on issues surrounding supply chain and expense management categories, including airlines, hotels, meetings, ground transportation, corporate card programs, and travel management companies. Before founding her own consultancy in 2010, Scholar was with PricewaterhouseCoopers for thirteen years. In her last position there, she was lead for consulting with clients on Travel and Entertainment expenses.

Scholar is acknowledged nationally for groundbreaking efforts in shaping the SMM industry and integrating Travel and Meetings teams with Procurement. She is also an expert in driving virtual meeting adoption, both to reduce T&E costs and complement face-to-face events. (In 2002, she became the first meeting director to include virtual meetings under her direction.)

Among her industry activities, Scholar was a trustee of the GBTA Foundation and was co-chair of the association's Groups & Meetings Committee for four years. To advance the SMM industry, Scholar has created a host of innovative tools and resources for travel and meetings professionals, and she supplies the industry with numerous publications via her blog (http://www.teplus.net).

In 2010, *Corporate & Incentive Travel* magazine recognized Scholar as one of four of SMM's Movers and Shakers, and, in 2008, the publication named her one of the Top 20 Changemakers who influenced the meetings management industry. *Business Travel News* also named her Best Meeting Practitioner in 2007. Among her many professional designations, Scholar also holds a Six Sigma Green Belt.

John Pino, *Chairman, CEO, Founder of i-Meet*

John Pino has more than thirty years of experience in the meetings and events industry, and is a pioneer in the field of meetings management technology. In his most current role, Pino is the chairman, CEO, and founder of i-Meet, a global professional and social network for people, on both the buyer and supplier sides, that plans and manages meetings and events. Pino founded i-Meet in 2008. Before creating i-Meet, Pino founded meetings management technology company StarCite, Inc. and led the company from 1999 to 2008 as chairman and CEO. Pino remains a director on StarCite's board.

Before founding StarCite, Pino was also president and CEO of Philadelphia-based McGettigan Partners. At McGettigan, which was purchased by Maritz Travel Co. Inc. in 2001, Pino directed growth and expansion of the company, helping it become one of the largest meetings management firms in the world. Pino is a four-time recipient of the Top 25 Most Influential Executives of the business travel industry award from *Business Travel News* and a three-time recipient of *Meeting News*'s 25 Most Influential People in the Meetings Industry award.

Andrew Menkes, *CEO and Chairman, Partnership Travel Consulting, LLC*

Andy Menkes has a thirty-year history in the travel industry, with a varied background in the airline, travel agency, and corporate travel management businesses. He started his career with TWA, where his management experience included serving as regional manager of Interline Sales and later as the first regional manager of Automation Marketing.

Menkes's travel agency background began when founded and became CEO of Priority Travel, Inc., a New York–based agency with international offices in London and Hong Kong. Menkes also served in various regional and executive positions with a number of travel agencies. He joined Republic New York Corporation in January of 1997 as its first vice president of Global Travel Management. Menkes has received recognition as the first travel manager to be accredited by ARC as a Corporate Travel Department.

In 1998, *Business Travel News* named him one of the Top 25 Most Influential Executives of the business travel industry and in 1999, Travel Manager of the Year. He was once again recognized as one of the Top 25 Most Influential Executives in the travel industry, this time in 2000. Menkes founded Partnership Travel Consulting, LLC in 2001, a Princeton, NJ-based corporate travel consulting firm with a subsidiary based in the Netherlands.